TERRINE

Stéphane Reynaud

Φ

VEGETABLES

Vegetables make the perfect terrines … and not just for your vegetarian friends! A terrine packed with seasonal vegetables and herbs is guaranteed to delight all tastes and will bring welcome colour to your table.

Vegetable cream terrine

Serves 6
Preparation time: 40 minutes
Cooking time: 1 hour

100 g / 3 ½ oz carrots, sliced
100 g / 3 ½ oz cauliflower florets
5 eggs
500 ml / 18 fl oz (2 ¼ cups) double (heavy) cream
100 g / 3 ½ oz (1 cup) red cabbage, shredded
100 g / 3 ½ oz broccoli florets
100 g / 3 ½ oz pumpkin or other squash
salt and pepper

Cook the carrots and cauliflower in separate pans of boiling water until tender, then drain and put into separate bowls. Blend the carrots, one egg and 100 ml / 3 ½ fl oz (scant ½ cup) of the cream with a hand-held blender and season with salt and pepper. Blend the cauliflower, one egg and 100 ml /3 ½ fl oz (scant ½ cup) of the remaining cream with a hand-held blender and season with salt and pepper. Blanch the cabbage in salted boiling water, then drain, refresh under cold water, drain again and tip into a bowl. Blend with one egg and 100 ml/3 ½ fl oz (scant ½ cup) of the remaining cream with a hand-held blender and season with salt and pepper.

Blanch the broccoli in salted boiling water, then drain, refresh under cold water, drain again and tip into a bowl. Blend with one egg and 100 ml /3 ½ fl oz (scant ½ cup) of the remaining cream and season with salt and pepper. Cook the pumpkin, unpeeled, in boiling water. Remove from the pan, discard any seeds and scoop out the flesh into a bowl. Blend with one egg and the remaining cream with a hand-held blender and season with salt and pepper. Arrange alternate layers of the vegetable creams in a sterilized preserving jar and seal. Put the jar into a pan, pour in water to cover completely, place a weight on top to keep the jar submerged and bring to the boil. Lower the heat to a slow boil and cook for 1 hour. Remove from the pan and leave to cool.

Ratatouille terrine

Serves 6
Preparation time: 5 minutes or 2 hours
Cooking time: 40 minutes

Ratatouille
1 kg / 2 ¼ lb leftover ratatouille or:
6 tablespoons olive oil
2 courgettes (zucchini), diced
3 onions, diced
2 aubergines (eggplants), diced
4 tomatoes, diced
3 garlic cloves chopped

4 eggs
300 ml / ½ pint (1 ¼ cups) double (heavy) cream
pinch of ground cardamom
pinch of curry powder
1 teaspoon pastis
2 fresh basil sprigs, finely chopped
2 fresh tarragon sprigs, finely chopped
salt and pepper

If you are not using leftover ratatouille, preheat the oven to 200°C / 400°F / Gas Mark 6. Heat the olive oil in a flameproof casserole, add all the vegetables and the garlic and cook over a low heat, stirring occasionally, for 5 minutes. Cover the casserole, transfer to the oven and bake, stirring frequently, for 1 ½ hours. Remove from the oven and leave to cool. Preheat the oven to 180°C / 350°F / Gas Mark 4. Whisk the eggs with the cream in a bowl and stir in the cardamom, curry powder, pastis and herbs. Add the mixture to the leftover or cooled ratatouille and season with salt and pepper.

Line a terrine with cling film (plastic wrap), allowing it to overhang the sides, spoon in the ratatouille mixture and wrap the overhanging cling film over the top to seal. Put the terrine into a roasting tin (roasting pan), pour in boiling water to come about halfway up the sides and bake for 40 minutes, until the tip of a knife inserted into the centre comes out clean. Turn out and remove the cling film before serving. Serve warm or cold.

Artichoke and porcini terrine

Serves 6
Preparation time: 20 minutes
Standing time: 3 hours

juice of ½ lemon
12 frozen artichoke hearts, thawed
100 ml / 3 ½ fl oz (scant ½ cup) olive oil
2 garlic cloves, crushed
250 g / 9 oz frozen porcini mushrooms, thawed and sliced
1 tablespoon pine nuts
4 fresh parsley sprigs, coarsely chopped
400 g / 14 oz canned tomato confit slices
salt and pepper

Bring a pan of salted water to the boil and stir in the lemon juice. Add the artichoke hearts and cook for 10 minutes, until just tender, then drain well. Meanwhile, heat the olive oil in a frying pan (skillet), add the garlic and cook over a low heat, stirring occasionally, for a few minutes, until golden. Remove the garlic from the pan and set aside. Add the porcini to the pan and cook, stirring occasionally, for 7–8 minutes, until they have released all their liquid and have caramelized. Add the pine nuts and cook for about 1 minute more, until browned.

Mix together the porcini, pine nuts, garlic and parsley in a bowl and season with salt and pepper. Make alternating layers of tomato confit, artichoke hearts and the porcini mixture in individual ramekins. Press down well and chill in the refrigerator for 3 hours. Turn out the terrines onto individual serving dishes before serving.

Vegetable and cereal terrine

Serves 6
Preparation time: 30 minutes
Standing time: 3 hours

3 courgettes (zucchini), quartered lengthways
3 carrots, halved lengthways
2 tablespoons olive oil
1 onion, sliced
1 teaspoon coriander seeds, coarsely crushed
5 tablespoons white wine
1 fresh thyme sprig
1 bay leaf
½ fennel bulb, sliced
100 g / 3 ½ oz button mushrooms, quartered
juice of 1 lemon
3 gelatine (gelatin) leaves
300 ml / ½ pint (1 ¼ cups) vegetable stock
150 g / 5 oz (generous ¾ cup) cooked lentils
150 g / 5 oz (1 cup) cooked bulghar wheat
salt and pepper

Scoop out the cores from the courgettes. Using a sharp knife, cut the courgettes and carrots into 2-cm / ¾-inch chunks and then into ovals. Heat the olive oil in a pan, add the onion, cover and cook over a low heat, stirring occasionally, for about 5 minutes, until softened but not coloured. Add the coriander seeds, wine, thyme and bay leaf. Add the carrots, re-cover the pan and cook for 3 minutes. Add the fennel, re-cover the pan and cook for a further 3 minutes, then add the mushrooms, courgettes and lemon juice. Season with salt and pepper, remove the pan from the heat and leave the vegetables to cool in their cooking juices.

Pour a little cold water into a small bowl, add the gelatine and leave to soften for 5 minutes. Meanwhile, heat the vegetable stock in a pan. Squeeze out the gelatine and add to the stock, whisking constantly, then remove from the heat. Drain the cooled vegetables, reserving the cooking juices. Make layers of the vegetables, lentils and bulghar wheat in a terrine. Mix the reserved cooking juices with the stock and pour into the terrine. Chill in the refrigerator for 3 hours.

Terrine of baby leeks

Serves 6
Preparation time: 1 hour
Standing time: 24 hours

1 kg / 2 ¼ lb baby leeks
3–4 tablespoons olive oil
6 brown onions, cut into quarters
4 carrots, sliced
1 celery stick (stalk), cut into short lengths
¼ celeriac (celery root), coarsely chopped
2 garlic cloves, unpeeled
4 gelatine (gelatin) leaves
2 red onions, thinly sliced
salt and pepper

Cut off the green parts of the leeks and discard the top third. Slice the white parts of the leeks lengthways to within 2 cm / ¾ inch of the top and rinse thoroughly under cold running water. Pour enough olive oil into a pan to coat the base and heat. Add the green parts of the leeks, onion quarters, carrots, celery, celeriac and garlic cloves and cook over a low heat, stirring occasionally, for about 5 minutes, until the green parts of the leeks have softened. Pour in 2 litres / 3 ½ pints water (scant 8 ¾ cups), add the sliced leeks and cook for 15 minutes, until they are tender. Remove the sliced leeks from the pan and drain well. Bring the vegetable stock to the boil and cook until reduced, then season with salt and pepper.

Pour a little water into a small bowl, add the gelatine and leave to soften for 5 minutes. Meanwhile, strain the stock into a clean pan, pressing the vegetables down to squeeze out as much liquid as possible, then bring back to the boil. Squeeze out the gelatine and add to the stock, whisking constantly, then remove from the heat. Make layers of leeks and red onions in a rectangular terrine and pour in the vegetable stock to cover. Cover and chill in the refrigerator for 24 hours, until set. Before serving, warm the terrine very slightly so that it is easier to turn out.

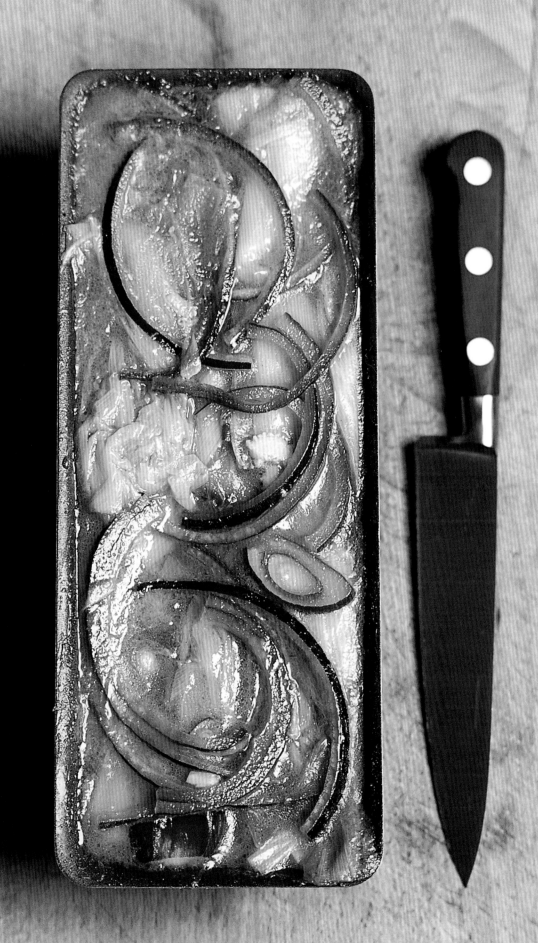

Summer terrine

Serves 6
Preparation time: 20 minutes
Cooking time: 40 minutes

1 kg / 2 ¼ lb courgettes (zucchini)
1 tablespoon coarse salt
5 tablespoons olive oil
4 eggs
200 ml / 7 fl oz (scant 1 cup) double (heavy) cream
1 bunch of fresh basil, chopped
pinch of green aniseed
pinch of ground cumin
salt and pepper

Using a vegetable peeler, slice two courgettes lengthways into thin strips, cutting as far as the core. Bring a pan of water to the boil and stir in the coarse salt. Add the courgette strips and blanch for 15 seconds, then drain and refresh in iced water. Drain again. Preheat the oven to 180°C / 350°F /Gas Mark 4. Cut the remaining courgettes in four lengthways and remove the cores, then dice. Heat the olive oil in a pan, add the diced courgettes and cook over a low heat, stirring occasionally, for about 5 minutes, until softened but not coloured. Lightly beat the eggs with the cream, basil, aniseed and cumin, stir in half the diced courgettes and season with salt and pepper. Add the remaining diced courgettes to the mixture.

Line a terrine with overlapping courgette strips and add the courgette mixture. Cover the terrine, put it into a roasting tin (roasting pan), pour in boiling water to come about halfway up the sides and bake for about 40 minutes, until the tip of a knife inserted into the centre comes out clean. Serve the terrine warm or cold.

Carrot, cumin and sesame terrine

Serves 6
Preparation time: 30 minutes
Cooking time: 10 minutes + 40 minutes

1 kg / 2 ¼ lb carrots, sliced lengthways into strips
5 eggs
400 ml / 14 fl oz (1 ¾ cups) double (heavy) cream
pinch of saffron threads
pinch of curry powder
1 teaspoon cumin seeds
1 ½ tablespoons white sesame seeds
salt and pepper

Preheat the oven to 180°C / 350°F / Gas Mark 4. Bring
a pan of water to the boil, add the carrot strips and cook
until tender but still firm to the bite. Mix together the eggs,
cream, saffron and curry powder in a bowl and season.
Line a terrine with cling film (plastic wrap), allowing it to
overhang the sides. Layer the carrots in the terrine, sprinkle
with the cumin and pour in the egg and cream mixture.
Wrap the overhanging cling film over the top to seal and
place the terrine in a roasting tin (roasting pan). Pour in
boiling water to come about halfway up the sides and bake
for 40 minutes. Meanwhile, dry-fry the sesame seeds in
a non-stick pan over a low heat for a few minutes, then
remove from the heat and set aside. Remove the terrine
from the roasting tin and leave to cool, then turn out,
remove the cling film, and sprinkle with the sesame seeds.

Tomato, basil and black olive terrine

Serves 6
Preparation time: 20 minutes
Standing time: 2 hours

1.2 kg / 2 ½ lb large tomatoes
150 g / 5 oz (1 ¼ cups) stoned (pitted) black olives
3 salted anchovies
1 garlic clove
dash of brandy
100 ml / 3 ½ fl oz (scant ½ cup) olive oil
1 bunch of fresh basil
salt and pepper

Cut out the stems from the tomatoes. Plunge the tomatoes
into boiling water for a few seconds, then drain and refresh
in iced water. Peel off the skins. Cut into quarters, remove
and discard the cores and set the flesh aside. Mix together
the olives, anchovies, garlic and brandy in a bowl, add the
olive oil and season with salt and pepper. Put the tomatoes,
basil leaves and olive mixture in individual ramekins, press
down firmly and set aside in a cool place for 2 hours. Turn
the terrines out before serving.

Red, green and yellow terrine

Serves 6
Preparation time: 30 minutes
Cooking time: 1 hour (if preserving)
Standing time: 24 hours

2 red peppers (bell peppers)
2 green peppers (bell peppers)
2 yellow peppers (bell peppers)
extra virgin olive oil, for drizzling
2 garlic cloves, thinly sliced
1 fresh thyme sprig
1 bay leaf
sea salt and peppercorns

Preheat the oven to 220°C / 425°F / Gas Mark 7. Put the
peppers on a baking sheet (cookie sheet), drizzle with olive
oil and roast, turning occasionally, for about 15 minutes,
until the skins start to blacken and char. Using tongs,
put the peppers into a plastic bag and tie the top. When
they are cool enough to handle, remove the stems, skins
and seeds and coarsely crush the flesh with a rolling pin.
Arrange alternate layers of the different colour peppers,
garlic, sea salt and peppercorns in a sterilized preserving
jar. Add the thyme and bay leaf, cover and leave to
marinate in the refrigerator for 24 hours. You can preserve
this terrine by covering the sterilized jar with boiling water
and boiling for 1 hour.

Quinoa, green olive and tomato confit terrine

Serves 6
Preparation time: 40 minutes
Standing time: 24 hours

4 tablespoons olive oil
2 shallots, chopped
1 preserved lemon, rinsed and diced
200g / 7 oz (1 cup) quinoa
3 gelatine (gelatin) leaves
100 ml / 3 ½ fl oz (scant ½ cup) medium-dry white wine
200 ml / 7 fl oz (scant 1 cup) vegetable stock
400 g / 14 oz canned tomato confit slices
100 g /3 ½ oz (scant 1 cup) stoned (pitted) green olives, sliced
salt and pepper

Heat the oil in a pan. Add the shallots and lemon and cook over a low heat, stirring occasionally, for about 5 minutes, until softened. Stir in the quinoa and cook, stirring constantly, for 2–3 minutes, until the grains are well coated in oil. Pour in water to cover, bring to the boil and simmer gently for about 15 minutes, until the liquid has evaporated and the grains are tender but slightly crunchy. Season with salt and pepper. Pour a little water into a small bowl, add the gelatine and leave to soften for 5 minutes. Meanwhile, pour the wine and vegetable stock into a pan and bring to the boil. Squeeze out the gelatine leaves and add to the pan, whisking constantly, then remove from the heat.

Make alternating layers of tomato confit, quinoa and olives in individual ramekins. Pour in the wine and stock mixture and leave to cool, then chill in the refrigerator for 24 hours, until set. Before serving, warm the terrine very slightly so that it is easier to turn out.

Thyme-flavoured terrine

Serves 6
Preparation time: 40 minutes
Cooking time: 40 minutes

6 aubergines (eggplants)
1 garlic clove
100 ml / 3 ½ fl oz (scant ½ cup) milk
pinch of grated nutmeg
3 fresh thyme sprigs, preferably flowering
300 ml / ½ pint (1 ¼ cups) double (heavy) cream
4 eggs
salt

Preheat the oven to 200°C / 400°F / Gas Mark 6. Prick the aubergines all over
with the tip of a knife, put them on a baking sheet (cookie sheet) and bake
for 20 minutes, until wrinkled. Cut them in half lengthways and scoop out the flesh,
reserving the skins. Put the garlic clove into a small pan, pour in the milk and
100 ml /3 ½ fl oz (scant ½ cup) water and simmer until tender. Drain and remove
the small green shoot. Preheat the oven to 180°C / 350°F / Gas Mark 4. Put
the aubergine flesh, garlic, nutmeg and thyme in a food processor or blender and
process until thoroughly combined. Add the cream and eggs, process briefly to
combine and season with salt.

Cut the reserved aubergine skins lengthways into 2-cm / ¾-inch strips. Use the
strips to line a terrine, arranging them in a lattice pattern and alternating the
outside and the inside of the skins. Spoon the aubergine mixture into the terrine,
cover and place in a roasting tin (roasting pan). Pour in boiling water to come
about halfway up the sides and bake for 40 minutes, until the tip of a knife inserted
into the centre comes out clean. Serve warm or cold.

Root vegetable terrine

Serves 6
Preparation time: 50 minutes
Standing time: 24 hours

3 leeks
2 onions
4 cloves
3 carrots
3 potatoes, quartered lengthways
3 parsnips, quartered lengthways
3 swedes (rutabagas), quartered lengthways
3 turnips, quartered lengthways
750 ml / 1 ¼ pints (3 cups) beef stock
3 gelatine (gelatin) leaves
salt and pepper

Cut off the green parts of the leeks and reserve. Stud each onion with two
cloves and slice the white parts of the leeks and the carrots, potatoes, parsnips,
swedes and turnips. Pour the beef stock into a pan, add the onions and the
green parts of the leeks and bring to the boil. Add all the remaining vegetables
and simmer for about 30 minutes, until tender. Remove the vegetables with
a slotted spoon and set aside. Bring the stock back to the boil and cook until
reduced, then remove from the heat. Season with salt and pepper and set
300 ml / ½ pint (1 ¼ cups) aside. Pour a little water into a small bowl, add the
gelatine and leave to soften for 5 minutes, then squeeze out and whisk into the
reserved hot stock.

Line a terrine with cling film (plastic wrap), allowing it to overhang the sides.
Make layers of leeks, carrots, potatoes, parsnips, swedes and turnips in the
terrine, pouring in the stock at intervals. Wrap the overhanging cling film on
top to cover and set aside in a cool place for 24 hours. Turn out and remove
the cling film before serving.

Spring vegetable terrine

Serves 6
Preparation time: 30 minutes
Cooking time: 40 minutes

100 g / 3 ½ oz (¾ cup) broad beans (fava beans)
1 tablespoon cooking salt
100 g / 3 ½ oz (scant 1 cup) petits pois (baby peas)
100 g / 3 ½ oz broccoli, cut into florets
100 g / 3 ½ oz green beans, cut into 1-cm / ½-inch lengths
100 g / 3 ½ oz new carrots, diced
100 g / 3 ½ oz (scant 1 cup) celery hearts, diced
4 eggs
300 ml / ½ pint (1 ¼ cups) double (heavy) cream
2 fresh tarragon sprigs
2 fresh basil sprigs, chopped
salt and pepper

Preheat the oven to 180°C / 350°F / Gas Mark 4. Pop the broad beans out of their skins by squeezing gently between your index finger and thumb. Bring a pan of water to the boil, stir in the cooking salt, add the petits pois and broccoli and blanch for 30 seconds. Remove from the pan, refresh in iced water and drain. Add the green beans, carrots and celery to the pan and cook for 5–10 minutes, until tender but still firm to the bite. Drain and refresh under cold water. Whisk the eggs with the cream in a bowl and add the petits pois, broccoli, green beans, carrots, celery, broad beans, tarragon and basil. Season with salt and pepper.

Line a terrine with cling film (plastic wrap), allowing it to overhang the sides. Spoon in the vegetable mixture, wrap the overhanging cling film over the top to seal and put the terrine into a roasting tin (roasting pan). Pour in boiling water to come about halfway up the sides and bake for 40 minutes, until the tip of a knife inserted into the centre comes out clean. Turn out and remove the cling film before serving. Serve warm or cold.

Minestrone terrine

Serves 6
Preparation time: 30 minutes
Standing time: 3 hours

1 bunch of green asparagus
1 courgette (zucchini)
100 g / 3 ½ oz (¾ cup) broad beans (fava beans)
2 tomatoes
300 ml / ½ pint (1 ¼ cups) vegetable stock
1 fennel bulb, thinly sliced
100 g / 3 ½ oz (scant 1 cup) petits pois (baby peas)
50 g / 2 oz spaghetti, broken into 1-cm / ½-inch lengths
1 shallot, chopped
1 bunch of fresh basil, chopped
3 gelatine (gelatin) leaves
3 fresh basil sprigs
salt and pepper

Trim the asparagus spears to 4 cm / 1 ½ inches and thinly slice lengthways.
Quarter the courgette lengthways, remove and discard the core and dice
the flesh into 5-mm / ¼-inch cubes. Pop the broad beans out of their skins
by gently squeezing them between your index finger and thumb. Cut out
the tomato stems and plunge the tomatoes into a pan of boiling water for
a few seconds, then remove and refresh in iced water. Peel off the skins and
dice the flesh into 5-mm / ¼-inch cubes. Bring the vegetable stock to the boil
in a pan. Add the fennel and cook until just tender but still firm to the bite,
then remove from the pan. In turn, cook the courgette, petits pois, broad beans
and spaghetti until just tender but still firm to the bite. Mix together the fennel,
courgette, petits pois, broad beans, tomatoes, spaghetti, shallot and chopped
basil in a bowl and season with salt and pepper.

Line individual terrines with cling film (plastic wrap) and then line them with
the sliced asparagus spears placed side by side. Spoon the vegetable mixture
into the centre. Pour a little water into a small bowl, add the gelatine and leave
to soften for 5 minutes. Meanwhile, bring the vegetable stock back to the boil.
Squeeze out the gelatine and add it to the stock, whisking constantly, then
remove the pan from the heat. Divide the stock among the terrines, then chill in
the refrigerator for 3 hours until set. Carefully remove the terrines from their
containers, using the cling film to help you, then discard the cling film before
serving. Use the basil leaves to decorate the tops of the terrines.

Cauliflower and red & green cabbage terrine

Serves 6
Preparation time: 20 minutes
Cooking time: 40 minutes

6 green cabbage leaves
1 cauliflower, cut into florets
4 tablespoons olive oil
2 shallots, sliced
¼ red cabbage, shredded
4 eggs
400 ml / 14 fl oz (1 ¾ cups) double (heavy) cream
salt and pepper

Preheat the oven to 180°C / 350°F / Gas Mark 4. Bring a pan of water to the boil, add the green cabbage leaves and blanch for 30 seconds, then remove from the pan and refresh in iced water. Add the cauliflower to the pan and cook for about 10 minutes, until tender, then drain. Meanwhile heat the olive oil in a large frying pan (skillet). Add the shallots and red cabbage and cook over a low heat, stirring occasionally, for about 5 minutes, until softened. Season with salt and pepper and remove from the heat. Put the cauliflower, eggs and cream in a food processor or blender and process until smooth and thoroughly combined. Transfer to a bowl and season with salt and pepper.

Line a terrine with cling film (plastic wrap), letting it overhang the sides, then line with the green cabbage leaves. Spoon in half the cauliflower mixture, add the red cabbage mixture and spoon the remaining cauliflower mixture on top. Wrap the overhanging cling film over the top to seal. Put the terrine into a roasting tin (roasting pan), pour in boiling water to come about halfway up the sides and bake for 40 minutes, until the tip of a knife inserted into the centre comes out clean. Turn out and remove the cling film before serving. Serve warm or cold.

SAUCES
for the vegetable terrines

Fried garlic, tomato and onion coulis

1 onion, halved
4 garlic cloves
3 tablespoons olive oil
50 g / 2 oz fresh root ginger, finely chopped
3 ripe tomatoes, diced
1 tablespoon tomato ketchup
1 teaspoon caster (superfine) sugar
salt and pepper

Finely chop half the onion and 3 of the garlic cloves. Heat 2 tablespoons of the oil in a pan. Add the ginger, chopped onion and garlic and cook over a low heat, stirring, for 10 minutes, until lightly browned. Add the tomatoes and cook, stirring, for 15–20 minutes, until pulpy. Cut the remaining garlic into small wedges and slice the remaining onion. Heat the remaining oil in a frying pan (skillet) and cook the garlic and onion over a low heat, stirring, for 10 minutes, until golden brown. Add the ketchup and sugar to the coulis, season with salt and pepper, and pour into a serving dish. Garnish with the garlic and onion mixture.

Curry cream

3 tablespoons double (heavy) cream
1 teaspoon curry powder
pinch of saffron threads
pinch of piment d'Espelette or
    other hot dried chilli (chile)
salt

Mix the cream, curry powder, saffron and chilli together in a bowl to obtain a light mousse-like consistency. Season to taste with salt.

Chive and shallot cream

2 tablespoons double (heavy) cream
1 tablespoon olive oil
1 teaspoon chopped shallot
1 tablespoon chopped chives
dash of Tabasco sauce
salt and pepper

Mix the cream, oil, shallot, chives and Tabasco together in a bowl and season to taste with salt and pepper.

Basil coulis

1 bunch of fresh basil
250 ml / 8 fl oz (1 cup) olive oil
juice of 1 lemon
salt and pepper

Remove the basil leaves from their stems and mix them with the olive oil and lemon juice in a bowl. Season to taste with salt and pepper.

FISH

Rich in fibre and vitamins, low in fat and high in protein, fish and seafood can be used to create healthy and delicious terrines and pâtés and to bring an element of sophistication to any menu.

Red mullet terrine

Serves 6
Preparation time: 20 minutes
Cooking time: 20 minutes

6 red mullet fillets, thawed if frozen
400 g / 14 oz white fish fillet, such as cod or whiting
20 g / ¾ oz (scant ½ cup) dried morel mushrooms
1 lemon
100 g / 3 ½ oz (¾ cup) broad beans (fava beans)
4 eggs
200 ml / 7 fl oz (scant 1 cup) double (heavy) cream
salt and pepper

Remove any remaining bones from the fish with tweezers. Skin and coarsely chop the white fish fillet. Put the dried morels in a bowl, pour in boiling water to cover and leave to soak for 15 minutes. Preheat the oven to 180°C / 350°F / Gas Mark 4. Pare thin strips of lemon zest with a citrus zester or sharp knife, blanch in boiling water for a few minutes, then drain. Squeeze the juice from half the lemon. Drain the morels. Pop the broad beans out of their skins by gently squeezing them between your index finger and thumb. Put the white fish fillet, eggs, cream and lemon juice in a food processor or blender and process until combined. Scrape the mixture into a bowl and season with salt and pepper. Stir in the broad beans, morels and lemon zest.

Line a terrine with cling film (plastic wrap), allowing it to overhang the sides. Then line it with the red mullet fillets, skin against the film. Spoon in the white fish mixture and wrap the overhanging cling film over the top to seal. Put the terrine in a roasting tin (roasting pan), pour in boiling water to come about halfway up the sides and bake for 20 minutes. Remove from the roasting tin and leave to cool. Turn out and remove the cling film before serving.

Haddock and Puy lentil terrine

Serves 6
Preparation time: 40 minutes
Standing time: 3 hours

200 g / 7 oz haddock fillet
3 garlic cloves
300 ml / ½ pint (1 ¼ cups) milk
200 g / 7 oz (scant ½ cup) Puy lentils (French green lentils)
1 bouquet garni
1 carrot
5 tablespoons white wine
1 shallot, finely chopped
300 ml / ½ pint (1 ¼ cups) vegetable stock
1 red onion, finely chopped
1 bunch of fresh tarragon, chopped
1 teaspoon wholegrain mustard
100 ml / 3 ½ fl oz (scant ½ cup) olive oil
3 gelatine (gelatin) leaves
salt and pepper

Put the haddock and garlic cloves into a frying pan (skillet), pour in the milk and 300 ml / ½ pint (1 ¼ cups) water and bring to the boil. Lower the heat and simmer for 8–10 minutes, until the flesh flakes easily. Lift out the haddock with a fish slice (slotted spatula) and remove and discard the skin. Remove and discard any remaining bones and flake the flesh. Remove the garlic and mash to a purée. Put the lentils in a pan, pour in water to cover, add the bouquet garni and carrot and bring to the boil. Lower the heat and simmer for about 20 minutes, until tender but not disintegrating. Drain well, remove and discard the bouquet garni and carrot, and set the lentils aside. Bring the wine to the boil in a pan, add the shallot and cook until the liquid has reduced to three-quarters, then add the vegetable stock.

Mix together the lentils, haddock, red onion and tarragon. Mix the mustard with the olive oil and garlic purée in a small bowl, stir into the lentil and haddock mixture and season with salt and pepper. Add the mixture to six individual glasses or ramekins. Pour a little water into a small bowl, add the gelatine and leave for 5 minutes to soften. Meanwhile, bring the vegetable stock mixture back to the boil. Squeeze out the gelatine and add it to the stock, whisking constantly, then remove the pan from the heat. Pour the stock over the lentil and haddock mixture, cover and chill in the refrigerator for 3 hours. Serve in the glasses or ramekins.

Smoked halibut and horseradish terrine

Serves 6
Preparation time: 20 minutes
Cooking time: 40 minutes

3 black or Spanish radishes
300 g / 11 oz smoked halibut or smoked haddock fillet
400 ml / 14 fl oz (1 ¾ cups) double (heavy) cream
5 eggs
1 teaspoon grated horseradish
2 shallots, finely chopped
salt and pepper

Preheat the oven to 180°C / 350°F / Gas Mark 4. Using a vegetable slicer or peeler, cut wide strips from the black radishes, discarding the first slice of each. Skin the smoked fish, remove any remaining bones, and thinly slice the flesh. Mix together the cream, eggs, horseradish and shallots in a bowl. Season with salt and pepper, bearing in mind that the smoked fish is already salty.

Line a terrine with cling film (plastic wrap), allowing it to overhang the sides. Make alternating layers of black radish and smoked fish, adding the horseradish cream as you go. Wrap the overhanging cling film over the top to seal. Put the terrine in a roasting tin (roasting pan), pour in boiling water to come about halfway up the sides and bake for 40 minutes. Turn out and remove the cling film before serving. Serve warm or cold.

Salmon terrine with ginger

Serves 6
Preparation time: 30 minutes
Cooking time: 40 minutes

300 g / 11 oz salmon fillet
300 g / 11 oz white fish fillet, such as whiting or cod
2 tablespoons olive oil
20 g / ¾ oz fresh root ginger, finely chopped
2 garlic cloves, finely chopped
4 eggs
300 ml / ½ pint (1 ¼ cups) double (heavy) cream
1 lime
1 orange
4 fresh chives, chopped
salt and pepper

Skin the fish and remove any remaining bones with tweezers. Coarsely chop the flesh, keeping the two types of fish separate. Heat the olive oil in a small non-stick frying pan (skillet). Add the ginger and garlic and cook over a low heat, stirring occasionally, for a few minutes, until lightly browned. Remove from the pan and set aside. Preheat the oven to 180°C / 350°F / Gas Mark 4. Put the salmon, two eggs and half the cream into a food processor or blender and process until smooth and thoroughly combined. Transfer to a bowl. Put the white fish, remaining eggs and remaining cream into a food processor or blender and process until smooth and thoroughly combined. Transfer to another bowl. Pare thin strips of the lime and orange zest with a citrus zester or sharp knife and blanch briefly in boiling water. Drain and set aside. Squeeze the juice from half the lime and half the orange. Stir the garlic and ginger mixture and the chives into the bowl of white fish and season with salt and pepper. Stir the citrus zest and juice into the bowl of salmon and season with salt and pepper.

Line a terrine with cling film (plastic wrap), allowing it to overhang the sides. Fill the terrine with layers of the fish mixtures and wrap the overhanging cling film over the top to seal. Put the terrine in a roasting tin (roasting pan), pour in boiling water to come about halfway up the sides and bake for 40 minutes. Turn out the terrine and remove the cling film before serving. Serve warm or cold.

Fish loaf

Serves 6
Preparation time: 20 minutes
Cooking time: 40 minutes

600 g / 1 lb 5 oz white fish fillets, such as whiting or cod
3 tomatoes
2 tablespoons olive oil
2 garlic cloves, finely chopped
3 shallots, finely chopped
4 eggs
200 ml / 7 fl oz (scant 1 cup) double (heavy) cream
1 tablespoon tomato ketchup
1 bunch of fresh basil, chopped
salt and pepper

Preheat the oven to 180°C / 350°F / Gas Mark 4. Skin the fish and remove
any remaining bones with tweezers. Cut the flesh into large cubes. Cut out
the stems from the tomatoes, plunge the tomatoes into boiling water for
a few seconds, then refresh in iced water. Peel off the skins, quarter and seed
the tomatoes and finely dice the flesh. Heat the olive oil in a small frying
pan (skillet). Add the garlic and shallots and cook over a low heat, stirring
occasionally, for about 5 minutes, until softened and transparent. Remove
the pan from the heat. Put the fish, eggs and cream into a food processor or
blender and process until smooth and thoroughly combined. Transfer to
a bowl and season with salt and pepper. Stir in the onion and garlic mixture,
ketchup, basil and tomatoes.

Line a terrine with cling film (plastic wrap), allowing it to overhang the sides.
Spoon in the fish mixture and wrap the overhanging cling film over the top
to seal. Put the terrine into a roasting tin (roasting pan), pour in boiling water
to come about halfway up the sides and bake for 40 minutes. Turn out and
remove the cling film before serving. Serve warm or cold.

Terrine of fresh and smoked salmon with vegetable julienne

Serves 6
Preparation time: 45 minutes
Cooking time: 40 minutes

1 red pepper (bell pepper)
2 courgettes (zucchini)
1 carrot
300 g / 11 oz salmon fillet, skinned and cut into chunks
4 eggs
300 ml / ½ pint (1 ¼ cups) double (heavy) cream
300 g / 11 oz white fish fillet, such as whiting or cod,
    skinned and cut into chunks
1 lemongrass stalk, chopped
6 smoked salmon slices
salt and pepper

Preheat the oven to 220°C / 425°F / Gas Mark 7. Put the red pepper
on a baking sheet (cookie sheet) and roast, turning occasionally, for about
15 minutes, until blackened and charred. Using tongs, transfer the pepper
to a plastic bag and tie the top. When the pepper is cool enough to handle,
peel off the skin, remove the seeds and cut the flesh into very thin strips.
Cut the courgettes lengthways into very thin strips and remove and discard
the cores. Blanch in a pan of salted boiling water for 15 seconds, then remove
and refresh under cold water. Cut these strips lengthways into fine juliennes.
Cut the carrot into thin lengthways strips, blanch, refresh and cut into fine
juliennes in the same way. Reduce the oven temperature to 180°C / 350°F /
Gas Mark 4. Put the fresh salmon, two eggs and half the cream into a food
processor or blender and process until smooth and thoroughly combined.
Transfer to a bowl and season with salt and pepper. Put the white fish,
remaining eggs and remaining cream into a food processor or blender and
process until smooth and thoroughly combined. Transfer to a bowl, stir in
the lemongrass and season with salt and pepper.

Line a terrine with cling film (plastic wrap), allowing it to overhang the sides.
Make layers of the white fish mixture, vegetables, smoked salmon and the
fresh salmon mixture, then smoked salmon, the white fish mixture, vegetables,
smoked salmon and the fresh salmon mixture. Wrap the overhanging cling film
over the top to seal. Put the terrine into a roasting tin (roasting pan), pour
in boiling water to come about halfway up the sides and bake for 40 minutes.
Turn out and remove the cling film before serving. Serve warm or cold.

Langoustine terrine

Serves 6
Preparation time: 30 minutes
Cooking time: 1 hour

8 cooked langoustines
3 tablespoons olive oil
1 tablespoon pastis
175 ml / 6 fl oz (¾ cup) white wine
1 tablespoon broad beans (fava beans)
1 tablespoon petits pois (baby peas)
200 g / 7 oz cod fillet, skinned and cut into chunks
2 eggs
150 ml / ¼ pint (⅔ cup) double (heavy) cream
1 tablespoon soy sauce
salt and pepper

Remove the heads and claws from the langoustines and peel the tails. Set the tails aside and crush the heads, legs and claws with a rolling pin. Heat the olive oil in a pan. Add the crushed langoustine shells and cook over a low heat, stirring occasionally, for 5 minutes. Add the pastis, heat for a few seconds and ignite. When the flames have died down, pour in the white wine and 175 ml / 6 fl oz (¾ cup) water. Cook until reduced to 100 ml / 3 ½ fl oz (scant ½ cup). Strain the shellfish stock through a fine strainer into a bowl. Pop the broad beans out of their skins by gently squeezing them between your index finger and thumb. Blanch the broad beans and petits pois in salted boiling water for 30 seconds, then drain and refresh under cold water. Put the cod, eggs, cream, soy sauce and shellfish stock into a food processor or blender and process until smooth and thoroughly combined. Transfer to a bowl, season with salt and pepper and stir in the broad beans and petits pois.

Spoon the cod mixture into a sterilized preserving jar, alternating with the langoustine tails, and seal. Place the jar in a pan, add water to cover completely, place a weight on top to keep the jar submerged and bring to the boil. Lower the heat to a slow boil and cook for 1 hour. Serve warm or cold.

Salmon rillettes

Serves 4
Preparation time: 10 minutes
Standing time: 1 hour

2 tablespoons olive oil
175 g / 6 oz salmon fillet, skinned and cut into chunks
80 g / 3 oz (6 tablespoons) butter, softened
1 tablespoon thick crème fraîche
2 fresh tarragon sprigs, finely chopped
1 teaspoon chopped shallot
juice of ½ lemon
salt and pepper
sliced lemon, to garnish

Heat the olive oil in a frying pan (skillet). Add the salmon
and cook over a high heat for about 4 minutes, until opaque
but still slightly raw in the centre. Put the salmon and
70 g / 2 ¾ oz (5 ½ tablespoons) of the butter into a food
processor or blender and process until smooth and
thoroughly combined. Transfer to a bowl, stir in the crème
fraîche, tarragon, shallot and lemon juice and season.
Spoon the mixture into a terrine or individual ramekins,
making sure that there are no air bubbles. Garnish with
lemon slices. Melt the remaining butter over a low heat and
pour it over the terrine or ramekins. Chill in the refrigerator
for 1 hour before serving.

Shellfish bouillabaisse terrine

Serves 6
Preparation time: 20 minutes
Cooking time: 40 minutes

500 ml/18 fl oz (2 ¼ cups) fish soup
2 tablespoons olive oil
3 shallots, chopped
1 garlic clove, chopped
200 g/7 oz cooked shelled mussels, thawed if frozen
200 g/7 oz cooked shelled cockles or small clams,
    thawed if frozen
1 teaspoon fennel seeds
3 fresh dill sprigs, finely chopped
300 ml / ½ pint (1 ¼ cups) double (heavy) cream
5 eggs
salt and pepper

Preheat the oven to 180°C / 350°F / Gas Mark 4. Pour the
soup into a pan, bring to the boil and cook until reduced
by half. Remove from the heat. Heat the olive oil in a frying
pan (skillet). Add the shallots and garlic and cook over
a low heat, stirring occasionally, for about 5 minutes, until
softened and transparent. Add the shellfish and cook for
a few minutes, then stir in the fennel seeds and dill. Mix
the cream with the soup reduction, whisk in the eggs
and season. Spoon the shellfish mixture into a terrine, pour
in the fish cream and cover. Put the terrine in a roasting tin
(roasting pan), pour in boiling water to come about halfway
up the sides and bake for 40 minutes. Serve warm or cold.

Avocado and shellfish terrine

Serves 6
Preparation time: 30 minutes
Standing time: 20 minutes

3 fresh basil sprigs
100 ml / 3 ½ fl oz (scant ½ cup) olive oil
200 g / 7 oz cooked peeled prawns (shelled shrimp)
3 avocados
juice of 1 lemon
1 spring onion (scallion), finely chopped
juice of 1 lime
200 g / 7 oz crab meat
1 tablespoon double (heavy) cream
salt and coarsely ground black pepper

Strip the basil leaves from the stems and mix with the olive
oil in a bowl, then add the prawns and season with salt
and pepper. Peel, halve, stone and thinly slice the avocados.
Sprinkle the slices with the lemon juice. Mix the spring
onion with the lime juice in a bowl. Pat the crab meat dry
and remove any remaining cartilage. Mix together the crab
meat, spring onion mixture and cream in a bowl and season
with salt and coarsely ground black pepper. Make layers
of the marinated prawns, avocado slices and crab mixture
in individual round dishes or rings. Press down and chill in
the refrigerator for 20 minutes before turning out.

Crab and smoked salmon terrine

Serves 6
Preparation time: 30 minutes
Standing time: 1 hour

For the cocktail sauce
1 egg
1 teaspoon balsamic vinegar
150 ml / ¼ pint (⅔ cup) olive oil
1 teaspoon strong mustard
1 teaspoon tomato ketchup
dash of brandy
salt and pepper

300 g / 11 oz canned crab meat, drained
300 g / 11 oz smoked salmon, diced
3 fresh dill sprigs, chopped
1 teaspoon chopped shallot
2 tablespoons olive oil
200 g / 7 oz spinach, coarse stalks removed
salt and pepper

To make the cocktail sauce, whisk the egg with the vinegar and a pinch of salt, then gradually add the olive oil, 1–2 teaspoons at a time, whisking constantly. When about a quarter of the oil has been absorbed, add the remaining olive oil in a slow, steady stream, whisking constantly. Stir in the mustard, tomato ketchup and brandy and season to taste with salt and pepper. Pat the crab meat dry and remove any remaining cartilage. Mix the crab meat with the cocktail sauce to taste. Mix together the smoked salmon, dill and shallot in a bowl. Heat the olive oil in a frying pan (skillet). Add the spinach and cook over a low heat, turning occasionally, for a few minutes, until just wilted. Remove the pan from the heat, season with salt and pepper and leave to cool.

Make layers of the smoked salmon mixture, spinach and crab mixture in individual dishes. Press down well and chill in the refrigerator for 1 hour. Turn out the terrines before serving.

Terrine of scallops and vegetable julienne

Serves 6
Preparation time: 30 minutes
Cooking time: 30 minutes

12 prepared scallops with coral
400 g / 14 oz white fish fillets, skinned and cut into chunks
4 eggs
300 ml / ½ pint (1 ¼ cups) double (heavy) cream
6 fresh chives, chopped
2 tablespoons olive oil
200 g / 7 oz spinach, coarse stalks removed
1 carrot, cut into julienne strips
1 courgette (zucchini), cut into julienne strips
2 spring onions (scallions), cut into julienne strips
3 green asparagus spears, trimmed and cut into julienne strips
1 fennel bulb, cut into julienne strips
salt and pepper

Separate the coral from the whiter scallop flesh. Put the fish, coral, eggs and cream in a food processor or blender and process until smooth and thoroughly combined. Transfer to a bowl, stir in the chives and season with salt and pepper. Heat the olive oil in a frying pan (skillet). Add the spinach and cook over a low heat, turning occasionally, for a few minutes, until wilted.

Make a bed of some spinach on a flat plate, put the scallops on top with a little of the white fish mixture in between and shape into a roll. Cover a sheet of cling film (plastic wrap) with the remaining spinach; this should be the length of the scallop roll and one and a half times its diameter. Spread the remaining white fish mixture on the spinach, cover with the vegetable juliennes, place the scallop roll in the centre and wrap the cling film around to seal. Make a knot, pressing in each side of the cling film to make sure the roll is even. Wrap the roll in a second sheet of cling film to make sure that the terrine is watertight. Bring a large pan of water to the boil, add the roll, lower the heat and poach gently for 30 minutes. Unwrap the terrine and serve warm or cold.

Lentil and snail terrine

Serves 6
Preparation time: 40 minutes
Standing time: 3 hours

250 g / 9 oz (generous 1 cup) Puy lentils (French green lentils)
1 bouquet garni
1 onion
3 cloves
2 tablespoons duck fat
3 garlic cloves, finely chopped
3 shallots, chopped
36 canned large snails, preferably Burgundy snails
1 bunch of fresh parsley, finely chopped
2 tablespoons olive oil
3 gelatine (gelatin) leaves
300 ml / ½ pint (1 ¼ cups) vegetable stock
sea salt and pepper

Put the lentils in a pan and add the bouquet garni. Stud the onion with the
cloves, add to the pan and pour in water to cover. Bring to the boil, then lower
the heat and simmer for 15–20 minutes, until the lentils are tender but not
disintegrating. Meanwhile, melt the duck fat in a pan over a low heat. Season
with sea salt, add the garlic and one shallot and cook over a low heat, stirring
occasionally, for a few minutes, until softened. Add the snails and cook gently
for 20 minutes, taking care that they do not brown. Once the lentils are tender,
drain them, rinse in cold water and place in a bowl. Stir in the parsley,
remaining shallots and the oil and season with salt and pepper. Drain the snails.

Pour a little water into a small bowl, add the gelatine and leave to soften for
5 minutes. Meanwhile, bring the vegetable stock to the boil in a pan. Squeeze
out the gelatine and add it to the stock, whisking constantly, then remove the
pan from the heat. Spoon a layer of lentils into the bases of six individual
terrines. Divide the snails, shallot and garlic among them, cover with another
layer of lentils and pour in the vegetable stock. Chill in the refrigerator for
3 hours, until set. To serve, briefly dip the base of the terrines in hot water
and turn out.

Lobster and prosciutto terrine

Serves 6
Preparation time: 45 minutes
Cooking time: 30 minutes

3 celery sticks (stalks)
1 bouquet garni
2 carrots
3 onions
2 uncooked lobsters, thawed if frozen
300 g / 11 oz white fish fillet, such as whiting or cod
4 eggs
300 ml / ½ pint (1 ¼ cups) double (heavy) cream
pinch of curry powder
2 tablespoons olive oil
100 g / 3 ½ oz spinach, coarse stalks removed
4 thin slices of prosciutto or other dry-cured ham
salt and pepper

Put the celery, bouquet garni, carrots and onions in a large pan, cover with water and bring to the boil. Simmer for 30 minutes. Meanwhile, lay each lobster on a flat surface, grasp the abdomen with one hand and the head with the other and pull apart. Remove and reserve the claws. Slice the head in half lengthways and remove and reserve the coral. Add the tails and claws to the pan, bring back to the boil, lower the heat and cook the tails for 5 minutes and the claws for 7 minutes. Remove from the heat and lift out the lobsters, reserving the stock. Lay the tails flat, halve lengthways and lift out the meat from each half. Using the point of a knife, remove and discard the intestinal tract. Crack the claws with a heavy knife and remove the meat in large pieces. Using tweezers, remove any bones from the white fish fillet and cut into chunks.

Put the fish, eggs, cream and curry powder into a food processor or blender and process. Transfer two-thirds of the mixture to a bowl and season with salt and pepper, bearing in mind that prosciutto is already salty. Add the corals to the blender and process. Heat the oil in a frying pan (skillet). Add the spinach and cook over a low heat, stirring, until just wilted. Remove from the heat. Spoon onto cling film (plastic wrap) to make a 30 x 10-cm / 12 x 4-inch rectangle. Spoon the fish and coral mixture on top and place the lobster meat in the middle. Roll up, wrap tightly in the cling film and freeze for 10 minutes. Meanwhile, put the prosciutto slices on a sheet of cling film, overlapping them to make a rectangle the same size as previously. Spoon the remaining fish mixture over them. Remove and discard the cling film from the lobster roll and put the roll on the fish mixture. Roll up and knot each end. Wrap the roll in another sheet. Bring the pan of reserved stock to the boil, then lower the heat so that it is barely bubbling. Poach the lobster for 30 minutes. Remove from the cling film and serve warm or cold.

Thai terrine

Serves 6
Preparation time: 20 minutes
Cooking time: 30 minutes

3 tablespoons brown sugar
3 tablespoons lemon juice
3 garlic cloves, finely chopped
1 teaspoon grated fresh root ginger
2 bird's eye chillies (Thai chiles), seeded and finely chopped
3 tablespoons nam pla (Thai fish sauce)
600 g / 1 lb 5 oz white fish fillets, such as whiting or cod
5 eggs
400 ml / 14 fl oz (1 ¾ cup) crème fraîche
4 spring onions (scallions), coarsely chopped
150 g / 5 oz (1 ¼ cups) cooked peeled prawns (shelled shrimp)
salt and pepper

Mix together the sugar, lemon juice, garlic, ginger, chillies and nam pla in a bowl. Remove any remaining bones from the white fish fillets with tweezers and cut the flesh into chunks. Put the white fish, eggs and crème fraîche in a food processor or blender and process until smooth and thoroughly combined. Transfer to a bowl and stir in the spring onions and prawns. Stir the garlic and chilli mixture to make sure that the sugar has completely dissolved, then add it to the fish mixture. Season to taste with salt and pepper.

Spoon the mixture onto a sheet of cling film (plastic wrap) and roll to form a large sausage shape. Twist the ends of the cling film to make sure that the terrine is tightly sealed. Bring a large pan of water to the boil, then lower the heat so that it is barely bubbling. Add the terrine and poach for 30 minutes. Remove from the cling film and serve warm or cold.

Nathalie has culinary magic in her fingertips! She instinctively knows how to choose exactly the right ingredients and her elegant recipes make people come back to the restaurant again and again.

Nathalie's Anchovy terrine

Serves 6
Preparation time: 50 minutes

3 red peppers (bell peppers), halved and seeded
3 yellow peppers (bell peppers), halved and seeded
2 aubergines (eggplants), thinly sliced into rounds
4 tablespoons olive oil, plus extra for drizzling
3 onions, thinly sliced
6 garlic cloves, thinly sliced
36 marinated fresh anchovies
salt and pepper

Preheat the oven to 200°C / 400°F / Gas Mark 6. Put the peppers, cut side down, on a baking sheet (cookie sheet) and roast for about 20 minutes, until blackened and charred. Meanwhile, put the aubergines into a roasting tin (roasting pan), drizzle with olive oil and roast for 10–15 minutes, until translucent. Remove the aubergines from the oven and season with salt and pepper. Using tongs, transfer the peppers to a plastic bag and tie the top. When the peppers are cool enough to handle, peel off the skins. Heat the olive oil in a non-stick pan. Add the onions and garlic and cook over a low heat, stirring occasionally, for about 10 minutes, until lightly browned.

Make a layer of a pepper half, aubergine slice and garlic and onion in each of six individual round dishes. Drain the anchovy fillets and divide them among the dishes. Continue to fill the dishes by repeating the layers in reverse, ending with a pepper half.

Marie works like a Trojan in the kitchen – she is such a hard worker, and she loves recipes that are a challenge!

Marie's Clam terrine

Serves 6–8
Preparation time: 30 minutes
Cooking time: 1 hour

2 kg / 4 ½ lb live clams
600 ml / 1 pint (2 ½ cups) white wine
4 shallots, thinly sliced
1 fresh thyme sprig
1 bay leaf
600 g / 1 lb 5 oz white fish fillet, such as cod, cut into chunks
3 eggs
1.5 litres / 2 ½ pints (6 ¼ cups) double (heavy) cream
1 courgette (zucchini)
2 fresh tarragon sprigs
salt and pepper

Preheat the oven to 180°C / 350°F / Gas Mark 4. Rinse the clams under cold running water. Discard any with broken shells or those that do not shut immediately when sharply tapped. Pour the white wine into a pan and bring to the boil, add the shallots, thyme and bay leaf and cook until reduced by a quarter. Add the clams, cover the pan and cook for 4–5 minutes, until the shells have opened. Drain the clams, reserving the cooking liquid. Discard any clams that remain closed and remove the remainder from their shells. Strain the cooking liquid through a muslin-lined (cheesecloth-lined) strainer into a bowl and set aside.

Put the white fish and eggs in a food processor or blender and process until smooth and thoroughly combined. Add the cream and process again, then add the reserved cooking liquid. Process again, transfer to a bowl and season with salt and pepper. Finely dice the courgette, removing the core. Strip the leaves from the tarragon. Add the courgette, tarragon and clams to the fish mixture. Line a terrine with cling film (plastic wrap), allowing it to overhang the sides. Spoon in the fish mixture and wrap the overhanging cling film over the top to seal. Put the terrine in a roasting tin (roasting pan), add boiling water to come about halfway up the sides and bake for 1 hour. Turn out and remove the cling film before serving. Serve warm or cold.

Jean-Marc is a king of culinary improvisation – he is always on the look out for new tastes and ingredients to include in his dishes and he is never afraid to experiment.

Jean-Marc's Oyster terrine

Serves 6
Preparation time: 30 minutes
Standing time: 6 hours

36 live oysters
6 gelatine (gelatin) leaves
1 teaspoon pepper, preferably Sarawak pepper
500 ml / 18 fl oz (2 ¼ cups) milk
1 tablespoon hazelnut oil

You will need a special oyster knife with a broad wooden handle and a short strong blade for shucking the oysters. It is not safe to use a kitchen knife. For extra protection for your hands, wrap a tea towel (dish towel) around the hand that you will use to hold the oyster shell. Holding an oyster firmly, flat shell uppermost, insert the knife into the hinged edge of the shell and twist to prise the shells apart. Slide the blade along the inside of the upper shell to sever one of the ligaments holding the oyster meat in place. Remove the top shell. Slide the blade under the oyster meat to sever the ligament beneath it, taking care not to spill the juices. Open all the oysters in the same way, tip the juices into a pan and leave the meat in the half shells to produce a second batch of juice. Tip that into the pan.

Pour a little water into a small bowl, add the gelatine and leave to soften for 5 minutes. Meanwhile, bring the pan of oyster juice to the boil. Squeeze out the gelatine and add it to the pan, whisking constantly. Whisk in the pepper and remove the pan from the heat. Remove the oysters from the half shells and layer them in a terrine, adding the peppered juice to each layer. Set aside in a cool place for 6 hours. Meanwhile, preheat the oven to its lowest setting. Mix the milk with the hazelnut oil in an ovenproof dish and bake for 20 minutes. When serving the terrine, whisk the milk to a foam and coat the terrine with this emulsion.

My sister-in-law Véronique is the perfect host. She was born to cook and loves entertaining – she even prepares her terrines the day before her guests arrive so that she doesn't miss a minute of their conversation!

Véro's Swordfish terrine

Serves 6
Preparation time: 40 minutes
Standing time: 24 hours

3 tablespoons olive oil
500 g/1 lb 2 oz swordfish loin
300 g/11 oz (2 ¼ cups) broad beans (fava beans)
3 baby courgettes (baby zucchini), cut into julienne strips
2 carrots, cut into julienne strips
1 tomato, cut into julienne strips
1 fresh parsley sprig, chopped
1 fresh coriander (cilantro) sprig, chopped
1 fresh chive, chopped
3 spring onions (scallions), cut into julienne strips
pinch of fresh thyme flower
100 g / 3 ½ oz (½ cup) cooked short grain rice
3 gelatine (gelatin) leaves
juice of 1 lemon
salt and pepper

Heat the olive oil in a frying pan (skillet). Season the swordfish with salt and pepper, add it to the pan and sear on all sides, leaving the centre pink. Remove the fish from the pan. Pop the broad beans out of their skins by gently squeezing them between your index finger and thumb. Mix together the broad beans, courgettes, carrots, tomato, parsley, coriander, chive, spring onions, thyme flower and rice in a bowl and season with salt and pepper.

Spoon this mixture into the base of a terrine and place the swordfish on top. Pour a little water into a small bowl, add the gelatine and leave to soften for 5 minutes. Meanwhile, pour 300 ml / ½ pint (1 ¼ cups) water into a pan, add the lemon juice and bring to the boil. Squeeze out the gelatine and add to the pan, whisking constantly. Pour the mixture into the terrine and chill in the refrigerator for 24 hours before serving.

SAUCES
for the fish terrines

Gribiche

1 egg yolk
1 teaspoon white wine vinegar
150 ml / ¼ pint (⅔ cup) sunflower oil
100 ml / 3 ½ fl oz (scant ½ cup) olive oil
1 teaspoon mustard
1 hard-boiled egg, chopped
1 teaspoon capers
1 shallot, chopped
6 fresh chives, chopped
1 teaspoon lemon juice
salt and pepper

Whisk together the egg yolk, vinegar and a pinch of salt in a bowl. Gradually add the sunflower and olive oils, 1–2 teaspoons at a time, whisking constantly. When about a quarter of the oil has been incorporated, add it in a steady stream, whisking constantly. Stir in the mustard and season to taste with salt and pepper. Gently stir the hard-boiled egg, capers, shallot and chives into the mayonnaise and add the lemon juice.

Vinaigrette

2 tablespoons nam pla (Thai fish sauce)
2 tablespoons brown sugar
3 tablespoons sunflower oil
20 g / ¾ oz fresh root ginger, cut into thin sticks
2 tablespoons lemon juice
3 fresh coriander (cilantro) sprigs, chopped
3 garlic cloves, finely chopped
salt and pepper

Heat the nam pla in a small pan and stir in the brown sugar until dissolved. Remove the pan from the heat. Heat the sunflower oil in a small pan. Add the ginger and cook over a low heat, stirring occasionally, for a few minutes. Stir in the lemon juice and remove from the heat. Mix the nam pla and sugar, and the ginger and lemon juice together in a bowl with the coriander and garlic and season with salt and pepper.

Sauce vierge

1 lemon
3 tomatoes, peeled, seeded and diced
2 shallots, finely chopped
10 fresh chives, chopped
250 ml / 8 fl oz (1 cup) extra virgin olive oil
salt and pepper

Peel the lemon and cut out the segments from between the membranes with a sharp knife, then dice finely. Mix the segments with the tomatoes, shallots, chives and oil together in a bowl and season with salt and pepper.

Lime cream

4 tablespoons double (heavy) cream
finely grated zest and juice of 1 lime
1 teaspoon caster (superfine) sugar
½ shallot, finely chopped
salt and pepper

Put the cream, lime zest and juice and sugar into a food processor or blender and process until smooth and thoroughly combined. Transfer to a bowl, stir in the shallot and season with salt and pepper.

MEAT

*Classic meat, poultry and game terrines can be rustic or sophisticated,
luxurious or thrifty. In my native Ardèche, where the back of my
family's butcher's shop was my playroom, I was brought up eating
homemade terrine every day. My grandparents' kitchen reflected their
working life, and meat terrines of all types – whether made from pork,
veal, beef, duck, chicken or game – were always on the menu.
I have given the recipes for meat terrines by weight, as they can be
divided amongst your guests, depending on how many arrive.
If you are serving them as a light lunch, these terrines can easily feed
6 – 8 hungry people.*

Chicken terrine

Makes 1 kg / 2 ¼ lb
Preparation time: 20 minutes
Cooking time: 1 hour

3 tablespoons olive oil
3 shallots, chopped
3 garlic cloves, chopped
600 g/1 lb 5 oz skinless, boneless chicken breasts, diced
5 eggs
300 ml / ½ pint (1 ¼ cups) double (heavy) cream
pinch of grated nutmeg
6 fresh chives, chopped
salt and pepper

Preheat the oven to 180°C / 350°F / Gas Mark 4. Heat the olive oil in a frying pan (skillet). Add the shallots and garlic and cook over a low heat, stirring occasionally, for about 5 minutes, until softened and translucent. Remove the pan from the heat. Put the chicken and eggs into a food processor or blender and process until smooth and thoroughly combined. If you prefer, you can use turkey in place of chicken. Add the cream and nutmeg and process again.

Transfer to a bowl and stir in the shallots and garlic and the chives. Season with salt and pepper. Spoon into a terrine and cover. Put the terrine into a roasting tin (roasting pan), add boiling water to come about halfway up the sides and bake for 1 hour. Serve warm or cold.

Chicken liver terrine

Makes 1 kg / 2 ¼ lb
Preparation time: 30 minutes
Cooking time: 2 hours

1 tablespoon duck fat or other fat
2 onions, coarsely chopped
300 g / 11 oz chicken livers, trimmed
3 tablespoons brandy
100 g / 3 ½ oz (generous ½ cup) smoked bacon, diced
300 g / 11 oz boneless pork belly (side), coarsely minced (ground)
200 g / 7 oz boneless pork blade (shoulder), coarsely minced (ground)
2 shallots, chopped
1 teaspoon quatre épices
2 eggs
200 ml / 7 fl oz (scant 1 cup) double (heavy) cream
2 fresh thyme sprigs, chopped
salt and pepper

Preheat the oven to 200°C / 400°F / Gas Mark 6. Melt the fat in a frying pan
(skillet). Add the onions and cook over a low heat, stirring occasionally, for
5 minutes, until softened. Add the chicken livers and cook, stirring frequently,
for about 5 minutes, until browned. Pour in the brandy, heat for a few seconds
and ignite. When the flames have died down, remove the pan from the heat.

Mix the bacon with the minced pork in a bowl, add the chicken livers and onions,
shallots, spice, eggs, cream and thyme and mix well. Season with salt and pepper,
then spoon the mixture into a terrine and cover. Put the terrine into a roasting tin
(roasting pan), add boiling water to come about halfway up the sides and bake for
2 hours. Serve warm or cold.

Oxtail and red wine terrine

Makes 1 kg / 2 ¼ lb
Preparation time: 4 ½ hours
Standing time: 24 hours

2 kg / 4 ½ lb oxtails
2 onions
4 cloves
3 celery sticks (stalks)
1 bouquet garni
3 leeks
6 carrots
1 teaspoon coriander seeds, coarsely crushed
1 teaspoon coarsely ground black pepper
500 ml / 18 fl oz (2 ¼ cups) Cornas, Côtes du Rhône or other
    full-bodied red wine
1 teaspoon quatre épices
3 gelatine (gelatin) leaves
salt and pepper

Put the oxtails in a large pan, pour in water to cover and bring to the boil.
Skim off the foam that rises to the surface with a slotted spoon. Stud the onions
with the cloves and add to the pan with the celery, bouquet garni, leeks
and carrots. Lower the heat and simmer for about 3 hours, until the meat comes
away from the bone. Lift out the oxtails and remove the meat from the bones
while it is still warm. Remove the carrots and leeks from the pan, slice and set
aside. Remove and discard the onions, celery and bouquet garni. Bring the
cooking liquid back to the boil and cook until reduced.

Dry-fry the coriander seeds and pepper in a frying pan (skillet), stirring
frequently, for a few minutes, until they give off their aroma. Add the wine, heat
for a few seconds and ignite, gently shaking the pan until the flames die down.
Cook until the liquid has reduced by a quarter. Pour in 200 ml / 7 fl oz
(scant 1 cup) of the reduced cooking liquid, add the spice and season with salt
and pepper. Pour a little water into a small bowl, add the gelatine and leave
to soften for 5 minutes. Squeeze out the gelatine and add it to the pan, whisking
constantly, then remove the pan from the heat. Put the meat, carrots and leeks
into a terrine, pressing them down, and pour in the wine and stock mixture.
Chill in the refrigerator for 24 hours.

Chicken liver parfait

Makes 4 x 250 g / 9 oz ramekins
Preparation time: 40 minutes

4 tablespoons olive oil
4 shallots, chopped
600 g / 1 lb 5 oz chicken livers, trimmed
8 juniper berries, crushed, plus extra to garnish
3 tablespoons golden rum
300 ml / ½ pint (1 ¼ cups) white port
300 g / 11 oz (1 ⅓ cups) slightly salted butter
1 gelatine (gelatin) leaf
4 bay leaves
salt and pepper

Heat the olive oil in a frying pan (skillet). Add the shallots and cook over a low heat, stirring occasionally, for about 5 minutes, until softened. Add the chicken livers and cook, stirring frequently, for about 5 minutes, until lightly browned. Stir in the juniper berries. Stir in the rum and heat briefly, scraping up the sediment from the base of the pan, then ignite. When the flames have died down, pour in 100 ml / 3 ½ fl oz (scant ½ cup) of the port and cook until reduced to a syrupy consistency. Remove the pan from the heat. While the chicken liver mixture is still warm, put it into a food processor or blender with the butter and process until thoroughly combined. Season to taste with salt and pepper.

Spoon the mixture into four ramekins and leave to cool. Pour a little water into a bowl, add the gelatine and leave to soften for 5 minutes. Meanwhile, heat the remaining port in a pan, squeeze out the gelatine and add it to the pan, whisking constantly. Spoon the port mixture over each cold terrine and garnish with a bay leaf and a few juniper berries.

Rabbit terrine with tarragon

Makes 1 kg / 2 ¼ lb
Preparation time: 3 ½ hours
Standing time: 3 hours

2 pig's trotters (feet)
1 onion
2 cloves
1 bouquet garni
1 carrot
1 celery stick (stalk)
1 leek
1 teaspoon coriander seeds
1 teaspoon pastis
800 g / 1 ¾ lb (1 ¾ cups) boneless rabbit,
   cut into 1-cm / ½-inch cubes
1 shallot, chopped
1 bunch of fresh tarragon
salt and pepper

Place the pig's trotters in a large pan and pour in water to cover. Stud the onion with the cloves and add it to the pan with the bouquet garni, carrot, celery, leek and coriander seeds. Bring to the boil, lower the heat and simmer for 2 ½ hours. Lift out the vegetables, bouquet garni and pig's trotters with a slotted spoon. Add the pastis and rabbit to the pan and cook for 20 minutes. Remove the rabbit with a slotted spoon and set aside.

Bring the cooking liquid back to the boil and cook until reduced to 300 ml / ½ pint (1 ¼ cups), then remove from the heat. If you like, cut the meat from the bones of the pig's trotters. Mix together the rabbit, shallot, tarragon and meat from the pig's trotters, if using, in a bowl and season with salt and pepper. Spoon the mixture into a terrine and pour in the reduced cooking liquid. Chill in the refrigerator for 3 hours, until set.

Rabbit rillettes

Makes 1 kg / 2 ¼ lb rillettes
Preparation time: 3 ½ hours

3 tablespoons duck fat, plus extra for sealing
2 carrots, diced
3 shallots, chopped
1 celery stick(stalk), diced
200 g / 7 oz smoked bacon, cut into sticks
1.5-kg / 3 ¼-lb rabbit, cut into pieces
175 ml / 6 fl oz (¾ cup) white wine
1 calf's foot
1 tablespoon veal or chicken stock (bouillon) powder
    or 2 crumbled stock cubes
salt and pepper

Melt the duck fat in a large pan. Add the vegetables and cook over a low heat, stirring occasionally, for 5 minutes, until softened. Add the bacon and rabbit and cook, stirring frequently, for 5–10 minutes, until lightly browned. Pour in the wine and cook for a few minutes, scraping up the sediment from the base of the pan. Add the calf's foot and pour in water to cover. Bring to the boil, add the stock powder and cook over a low heat for about 2 ½ hours, stirring constantly until the meat comes away from the bones. Strain the liquid into a clean pan and return to the heat.

Cut the rabbit and the calf's foot meat from the bones and mash the vegetables with a fork. Boil the cooking liquid until reduced to 200 ml / 7 fl oz (scant 1 cup), then stir in the meat and vegetables and season with salt and pepper. Divide the mixture among individual terrines, tapping them on the work surface to make sure that there are no air bubbles. Cover with a layer of melted duck fat to seal. Serve cold.

Rabbit and nut terrine

Makes 1 kg / 2 ¼ lb
Preparation time: 45 minutes
Cooking time: 2 hours

50 g / 2 oz (scant ½ cup) sultanas (golden raisins)
50 ml / 2 fl oz (¼ cup) Armagnac
1 tablespoon duck fat
3 shallots, chopped
200 g / 7 oz boneless rabbit, cubed
300 g / 11 oz boneless pork throat or hand (arm shoulder),
    coarsely minced (ground)
200 g / 7 oz chicken livers, trimmed and coarsely minced (ground)
pinch of ground cinnamon
pinch of piment d'Espelette or other hot dried chilli (chile)
100 ml / 3 ½ fl oz (scant ½ cup) double (heavy) cream
50 ml / 2 fl oz (¼ cup) white port
50 g / 2 oz (½ cup) almonds
50 g / 2 oz (½ cup) pistachio nuts
50 g / 2 oz (½ cup) hazelnuts
salt and pepper

Preheat the oven to 180°C / 350°F / Gas Mark 4. Put the sultanas in a bowl,
pour in the Armagnac, top up with warm water and leave to soak. Melt the duck
fat in a frying pan (skillet). Add the shallots and cook over a low heat, stirring
occasionally, for about 5 minutes, until softened and translucent. Add the rabbit
and cook, stirring frequently, for 5–10 minutes, until light golden brown.
Remove the pan from the heat.

Mix the rabbit and shallots with the pork and chicken livers in a bowl and stir
in the cinnamon, chilli, cream and port. Season with salt and pepper. Drain
the sultanas and stir them into the mixture with the nuts. Spoon the mixture
into a terrine and cover. Put the terrine into a roasting tin (roasting pan), pour
in boiling water to come about halfway up the sides and bake for 2 hours.
Serve cold.

Marbled rabbit
and foie gras terrine

Makes 1 kg / 2 ¼ lb
Preparation time: 20 minutes
Cooking time: 30 minutes

2 garlic cloves
100 ml / 3 ½ fl oz (scant ½ cup) milk
800 g / 1 ¾ lb boneless rabbit, diced
3 eggs
300 ml / ½ pint (1 ¼ cups) double (heavy) cream
100 g / 3 ½ oz (scant ½ cup) walnuts, finely chopped
2 bacon strips
200 g / 7 oz fresh foie gras, cut into 1-cm / ½-inch sticks
1 litre / 1 ¾ pints (4 cups) vegetable stock
sea salt and pepper

Put the garlic cloves into a pan, pour in the milk, add 100 ml / 3 ½ fl oz
(scant ½ cup) water and cook for about 20 minutes, until tender. Remove
the garlic with a slotted spoon and put into a food processor or blender with
the rabbit, eggs, a pinch of pepper and the cream. Process until thoroughly
combined, season with sea salt and add the walnuts.

Lay out the strips of bacon on a sheet of cling film (plastic wrap) to form
a 25 x 15-cm /10 x 6-inch rectangle and spread the rabbit mixture evenly over
them. Put three rows of the foie gras at regular intervals along the whole
length. Roll up, wrap in the cling film and knot the ends to secure, then tie with
string at intervals. Bring the vegetable stock to the boil, then lower the heat so
that it is barely bubbling. Add the terrine and poach for 30 minutes. Remove
from the pan and leave to cool. Discard the cling film before serving.

Foie gras and artichoke terrine

Makes 1 kg / 2 ¼ lb
Preparation time: 45 minutes
Standing time: 2 hours
Cooking time: 30 minutes

300 g / 11 oz frozen artichoke hearts
juice of ½ lemon
800 g / 1 ¾ lb fresh or frozen foie gras
¼ teaspoon quatre épices
50 ml /2 fl oz (¼ cup) Banyuls or other sweet wine
salt and pepper

Put the artichoke hearts in a pan, pour in water to cover and add the lemon
juice. Bring to the boil, then lower the heat and simmer according to the
instructions on the packet until firm. Drain and season with salt and pepper.
If using a whole foie gras, prepare it as described on page 90 and season
with the spice and wine, and cut into slices. Make alternate layers of foie gras
and artichoke hearts in a terrine, press down well and set aside in a cool place
for 2 hours.

Preheat the oven to 110°C /225°F /Gas Mark ¼ and preheat a roasting tin
(roasting pan) half-filled with boiling water at the same time. Cover the terrine,
put it into the roasting tin and bake for 30 minutes. When cool, store the
terrine in the refrigerator.

Foie gras terrine with pain d'épice

Makes 1 kg / 2 ¼ lb
Preparation time: 30 minutes
Standing time: 24 hours

100 g / 3 ½ oz pain d'épice or other gingerbread, sliced
    (see page 132)
50 g / 2 oz (½ cup) hazelnuts
1 teaspoon coarsely ground black pepper
1 kg / 2 ¼ lb fresh or frozen foie gras,
    cut into 1-cm / ½-inch thick slices
salt

Preheat the oven to 140°C / 275°F / Gas Mark 1. Put the slices of gingerbread on a baking sheet (cookie sheet) and dry out in the oven for 10–15 minutes. Put the spice cake and hazelnuts in a food processor or blender and process until the mixture resembles fine breadcrumbs. Add the pepper. Preheat a non-stick frying pan (skillet), add the foie gras and cook over a high heat, turning once, for a few minutes, until lightly browned but still firm. Make alternate layers of foie gras and spice cake mixture in a terrine, seasoning each layer with salt. Press down and leave to stand in a cool place for 24 hours before serving.

Foie gras

Makes 1 kg / 2 ¼ lb
Preparation time: 30 minutes
Standing time: 2 hours + 24 hours
Cooking time: 30 minutes

1 kg / 2 ¼ lb fresh or frozen foie gras
4 teaspoons brandy
50 ml / 2 fl oz (¼ cup) white port
½ teaspoon quatre épices
2 teaspoons salt

To prepare the foie gras, separate the lobes, then, using a sharp knife, remove the nerves and all the veins. Keep the liver cool – it must not be reheated. Mix together the brandy and port in a bowl and drizzle the mixture over the liver. Season with the salt and add the spice. Press the liver into a terrine and set aside in a cool place for 2 hours. Preheat the oven to 110°C / 225°F / Gas Mark ¼ and preheat a roasting tin (roasting pan) half-filled with boiling water at the same time. Cover the terrine, put it into the roasting tin and bake for 30 minutes. Remove the terrine and leave it to stand, then press down the liver and spoon off and reserve the fat. Store in a cool place for 24 hours. Melt the reserved fat over a low heat. Skim off any scum that rises to the surface, then pour the fat into the terrine in a thin layer, leaving any impurities behind in the pan. Store the terrine in a cool place.

Foie gras, Sauternes and smoked duck breast terrine

Makes 1 kg / 2 ¼ lb
Preparation time: 30 minutes
Standing time: 24 hours

1 kg / 2 ¼ lb fresh or frozen foie gras
100 ml / 3 ⅓ fl oz (scant ½ cup) Sauternes or other
    dessert wine
1 teaspoon sugar
pinch of ground cinnamon
2 teaspoons sea salt
1 smoked duck breast
white pepper

Prepare the foie gras as described opposite. Mix the
liver with the Sauternes, sugar, cinnamon, salt and a pinch
of white pepper. Remove the fat from the duck breast and
halve the breast lengthways. Lay the foie gras on a sheet of
cling film (plastic wrap), put the duck breast halves in the
middle and roll up. Wrap tightly in the cling film, securing
the ends. The roll must be airtight. Leave to stand in a cool
place for 24 hours before serving.

Foie gras terrine with dried fruit and Armagnac

Makes 1 kg/2 ¼ lb
Preparation time: 45 minutes
Standing time: 2 hours
Cooking time: 30 minutes

50 g / 2 oz (¼ cup) stoned (pitted) prunes
50 g / 2 oz (¼ cup) dried apricots
1 tablespoon pistachio nuts
1 tablespoon hazelnuts
1 tablespoon almonds
50 ml / 2 fl oz (¼ cup) Armagnac
1 kg / 2 ¼ lb fresh or frozen foie gras
pinch of ground cinnamon
salt and pepper
sea salt and coarsely ground black pepper, to serve

Mix together the prunes, apricots, pistachios, hazelnuts, almonds and
Armagnac in a bowl. Spread out a sheet of cling film (plastic wrap) and
spoon the mixture on to it, shaping it into a roll the same length as the terrine.
Wrap with the cling film and roll the parcel backwards and forwards to make it
even. Tie the ends and place in the freezer. Prepare the foie gras as described
on page 90, lightly season with salt and pepper and sprinkle with a pinch
of cinnamon.

Line a terrine with half the foie gras. Unwrap the dried fruit roll and put it
into the centre, then cover with the remaining foie gras, pressing down well.
Leave to stand for 2 hours. Preheat the oven to 110°C / 225°F / Gas Mark ¼
and preheat a roasting tin (roasting pan) half-filled with boiling water at
the same time. Cover the terrine, put it into the roasting tin and bake for
30 minutes. When cold, store in the refrigerator. Serve this foie gras terrine
with sea salt and coarsely ground black pepper to create a contrast with the
sharp taste of the dried fruit.

Veal terrine with Muscat

Makes 1 kg / 2 ¼ lb
Preparation time: 3 ½ hours
Cooking time: 30 minutes

1 veal knuckle (shank)
3 calf's feet
1 bouquet garni
1 tablespoon veal or chicken stock (bouillon) powder
    or 2 crumbled stock cubes
200 ml / 7 fl oz (scant 1 cup) Muscat or other dry white wine
3 carrots, finely diced
2 celery sticks (stalks), finely diced
3 shallots, finely diced
salt and pepper

Put the veal knuckle, calf's feet, bouquet garni and stock powder in
a large pan, pour in water to cover and bring to the boil. Lower the heat
and simmer for 3 hours, until the meat comes away from the knuckle
bone. Lift out the knuckle and calf's feet from the pan. Preheat the oven
to 180°C /350°F /Gas Mark 4. Bring the cooking liquid back to the boil
and cook until reduced. Add the Muscat, bring back to the boil and cook
until further reduced again. Remove the pan from the heat, discard the
bouquet garni and season the stock with salt and pepper.

Cut the meat from the bones, chop coarsely and mix with the carrots,
celery and shallots. Spoon the mixture into a terrine without pressing
it down, pour in the stock and cover. Put the terrine into a roasting
tin (roasting pan), pour in boiling water to come about halfway up the
sides and bake for 30 minutes. Serve cold.

Terrine beaujolaise

Makes 1 kg / 2 ¼ lb
Preparation time: 30 minutes
Marinating time: 24 hours
Cooking time: 2 hours

300 g / 11 oz boneless pork throat or hand (arm shoulder), cut into cubes
300 g / 11 oz boneless pork blade (shoulder), cut into cubes
200 g / 7 oz pig's liver, cut into cubes
3 carrots, thinly sliced
4 onions, thinly sliced
4 garlic cloves, thinly sliced
1 bay leaf
400 ml / 14 fl oz (1 ¾ cups) Beaujolais
100 ml / 3 ½ fl oz (scant ½ cup) ruby port
1 pig's caul
salt and pepper

Mix together all the meat, the carrots, onions, garlic and bay leaf in a dish, pour
in the wine and port and leave to marinate for 24 hours. Soak the caul in cold
water and drain. Preheat the oven to 180°C / 350°F / Gas Mark 4. Drain the
meat and vegetables, reserving the marinade. Remove and discard the bay leaf.
Coarsely mince (grind) all the ingredients and season with salt and pepper.
Stir in half the reserved marinade.

Spoon the mixture into an earthenware terrine and cover with the caul, making
sure that the mixture is neatly covered at the edges. Put the terrine into
a roasting tin (roasting pan), add boiling water to come about halfway up
the sides and bake for 2 hours, until browned on top. Serve cold.

Pig's head pâté

Makes 1 kg / 2 ¼ lb
Preparation time: 4 ½ hours
Cooking time: 30 minutes
Standing time: 24 hours

2 pig's tongues
2 pig's trotters (feet)
2 pig's snouts
2 pig's ears
200 g / 7 oz pork blade (shoulder)
1 brown onion
3 cloves
1 bouquet garni
1 leek
2 carrots
1 fennel bulb
2 Spanish (yellow) onions, chopped
5 fresh parsley sprigs, chopped
salt and pepper

Put all the meat in a large pan, pour in water to cover, bring to the boil and
skim off the foam that rises to the surface with a slotted spoon. Stud the brown
onion with the cloves and add to the pan with the bouquet garni, leek, carrots
and fennel, then lower the heat and simmer for 3 ½ hours. Preheat the oven
to 180°C / 350°F / Gas Mark 4. Lift out the meat, bring the cooking liquid back
to the boil and cook until reduced to 400 ml / 14 fl oz (1 ¾ cups). Strain into
a bowl and reserve the carrots, leek and fennel.

Coarsely chop the tongues, snouts and ears. Cut the meat from the blade and
trotters. Slice the reserved carrots, leek and fennel and mix with the Spanish
onions, parsley and meat. Season with salt and pepper. Spoon the mixture into
a terrine and pour in the reduced cooking liquid. Cover and put the terrine
into a roasting tin (roasting pan), pour in boiling water to come about halfway
up the sides and bake for 30 minutes. Chill in the refrigerator for 24 hours
before serving.

Country-style terrine

Makes 1 kg / 2 ¼ lb
Preparation time: 40 minutes
Cooking time: 2 hours
Standing time: 48 hours

1 tablespoon caster (superfine) sugar
50 ml / 2 fl oz (¼ cup) rum
6 tablespoons olive oil
4 onions, coarsely chopped
4 shallots, coarsely chopped
3 garlic cloves, coarsely chopped
400 g / 14 oz boneless pork belly (side), minced (ground)
300 g / 11 oz boneless pork blade (shoulder), minced (ground)
300 g / 11 oz pig's liver, minced (ground)
2 eggs
100 ml / 3 ½ fl oz (scant ½ cup) double (heavy) cream
pinch of grated nutmeg
5 fresh parsley sprigs, chopped
2 fresh thyme sprigs
1 bay leaf
6–8 thin strips of bacon fat
salt and pepper

Preheat the oven to 180°C / 350°F / Gas Mark 4. Mix together the sugar and
rum in a small bowl, stirring until the sugar has dissolved. Heat the olive oil in
a large pan. Add the onions, shallots and garlic and cook over a low heat,
stirring occasionally, for about 10 minutes, until lightly browned. Stir in the rum
mixture, heat for a few seconds and ignite. When the flames have died down,
cook until the vegetables are caramelized, then remove the pan from the heat.

Mix together the meat, eggs and cream in a bowl and stir in the nutmeg. Add
the onions, shallots and garlic and season with salt and pepper. Mix the parsley
with the thyme leaves and stir in. Spoon the mixture into a terrine, put the
bay leaf on top and make a lattice pattern with the bacon fat. Put the terrine
into a roasting tin (roasting pan), pour in boiling water to come about halfway
up the sides and bake for 2 hours. Leave the terrine to stand for 48 hours
before serving. Serve cold.

Veal pâté in pastry

Makes 1 kg / 2 ¼ lb
Preparation time: 40 minutes
Marinating time: 1 hour
Cooking time: 1 hour

2 tablespoons olive oil
3 shallots, chopped
300 g / 11 oz boneless veal shoulder,
    trimmed and cut into 2-cm / ¾-inch cubes
300 ml / ½ pint (1 ¼ cups) white wine
4 teaspoons brandy
4 teaspoons rum
1 teaspoon quatre épices
400 g /14 oz shortcrust pastry (pie) dough, thawed if frozen
plain (all-purpose) flour, for dusting
100 g / 3 ½ oz boiled ham, coarsely chopped
200 g / 7 oz boneless veal scrag end (blade), minced (ground)
300 g / 11 oz streaky (fatty) bacon, minced (ground)
1 egg
1 egg yolk, lightly beaten
100 g / 3 ½ oz aspic made from aspic jelly (gelatin) powder
salt and pepper

Heat the olive oil in a frying pan (skillet). Add the shallots and cook over a
low heat, stirring occasionally, for 5 minutes, until softened but not coloured.
Remove the pan from the heat and set aside. Put the shoulder of veal into
a shallow dish. Mix together the white wine, brandy, rum and spice in a jug,
pour the mixture over the veal cubes and leave to marinate for 1 hour, then
drain. Preheat the oven to 180°C /350°F / Gas Mark 4. Line a terrine with
greaseproof (waxed) paper. Cut off and reserve one-third of the pastry dough.
Roll out the remainder on a lightly floured surface and use to line the terrine,
allowing it to overhang the sides by 1 cm / ½ inch all round. Season the
ham with salt and pepper and mix it with the minced meat, veal cubes, shallot
and whole egg in a bowl, then spoon the mixture into the terrine, pressing
down well.

Roll out the remaining pastry dough, brush the sides with egg yolk and cover
the terrine, pinching the edges together to seal. Brush the top with egg yolk.
Cut a slit in the top of the dough, roll up a small cone of greaseproof paper and
insert it to make a chimney to allow the steam to escape during cooking. Bake
the terrine for 1 hour, then remove from the oven and leave to cool completely.
Carefully pour the aspic into the terrine through the greaseproof paper
chimney. Leave to cool. Remove from the terrine and discard the greaseproof
paper before serving.

Meat loaf

Makes 1 kg / 2 ¼ lb
Preparation time: 30 minutes
Cooking time: 1 hour

3 tablespoons olive oil
3 celery sticks (stalks), diced
2 onions, diced
675 g / 1 ½ lb minced (ground) beef
2 eggs
200 ml / 7 fl oz (scant 1 cup) double (heavy) cream
50 ml / 2 fl oz (¼ cup) tomato ketchup
40 g / 1 ½ oz (½ cup) Parmesan cheese, grated
dash of Tabasco sauce
salt and pepper

Preheat the oven to 200°C / 400°F / Gas Mark 6. Heat the
olive oil in a frying pan (skillet). Add the celery and onions
and cook over a low heat, stirring occasionally, for
5 minutes, until softened. Remove the pan from the heat.
Mix the minced beef with the celery and onion mixture,
eggs, cream, ketchup, cheese and Tabasco in a bowl
and season with salt and pepper. Spoon the mixture into
a terrine, cover and put into a roasting tin (roasting pan).
Pour in boiling water to come about halfway up the sides
and bake for 1 hour. Serve warm.

Italian veal loaf

Makes 1 kg / 2 ¼ lb
Preparation time: 45 minutes
Marinating time: 2 hours
Cooking time: 2 hours

400 g / 14 oz boneless loin of veal
200 ml / 7 fl oz (scant 1 cup) white wine
1 bay leaf
200 g / 7 oz boiled ham
200 g / 7 oz boneless pork belly (side)
4 shallots
3 eggs, lightly beaten
200 ml / 7 fl oz (scant 1 cup) double (heavy) cream
100 g / 3 ½ oz Parmesan cheese shavings
50 g / 2 oz rocket (arugula)
salt and pepper

Preheat the oven to 180°C /350°F / Gas Mark 4. Cut half the veal loin into thin strips and put into a dish. Add the wine and bay leaf and leave to marinate for 2 hours. Coarsely chop the ham with the pork belly, shallots and remaining veal. Put into a bowl, stir in the eggs and cream and season with salt and plenty of pepper. Add the veal strips. Spoon one-third of the mixture into a terrine, cover with half of the Parmesan shavings and rocket, add half the remaining mixture, cover with the remaining Parmesan shavings and rocket and, finally, add the remaining mixture. Cover the terrine, put it into a roasting tin (roasting pan), pour in boiling water to come halfway up the sides and bake for 2 hours. Serve warm or cold.

Flemish meat terrine

Makes 1 kg / 2 ¼ lb
Preparation time: 30 minutes
Marinating time: 12 hours
Cooking time: 3 hours
Standing time: 24 hours

300 g / 11 oz boneless pork blade (shoulder),
    cut into 2-cm / ¾-inch cubes
300 g / 11 oz boneless rabbit, cut into 2-cm / ¾-inch cubes
300 g / 11 oz boneless veal shoulder, cut into 2-cm /
    ¾-inch cubes
100 g / 3 ½ oz pork rind, cut into 2-cm / ¾-inch cubes
4 carrots, coarsely chopped
2 onions, coarsely chopped
4 garlic cloves, coarsely chopped
10 juniper berries, lightly crushed
750 ml / 1 ¼ pints (3 cups) Belgian beer
4 gelatine (gelatin) leaves
salt and pepper

Put all the meat, carrots, onions, garlic, juniper berries and beer into a dish. Cover and marinate for 12 hours. Preheat the oven to 160°C / 325°F / Gas Mark 3. Pour water into a bowl, add the gelatine and soak for 5 minutes. Drain the meat and vegetables, pour the marinade into a pan and bring to the boil. Squeeze out the gelatine and add to the pan, whisking, then remove from the heat and season. Spoon the vegetables and meat into a terrine and pour in the marinade. Cover, put the terrine into a roasting tin (roasting pan), pour in boiling water to come halfway up the sides and bake for 3 hours. Stand for 24 hours before serving.

Hare terrine with Marc de Bourgogne

Makes 1 kg / 2 ¼ lb
Preparation time: 45 minutes
Marinating time: 24 hours
Cooking time: 2 hours

500 g / 1 lb 2 oz hare meat, including a boned saddle
50 ml / 2 fl oz (¼ cup) Marc de Bourgogne or Burgundy
200 ml / 7 fl oz (scant 1 cup) Bourgogne Aligoté or Chardonnay
1 bay leaf
2 carrots, diced
300 g / 11 oz boneless pork blade (shoulder), diced
200 g / 7 oz boneless pork belly (side), diced
2 garlic cloves
2 shallots
pinch of savory
1 fresh rosemary sprig
2 fresh thyme sprigs
3 fresh parsley sprigs
150 ml / ¼ pint (⅔ cup) double (heavy) cream
10 thin smoked pork belly (side) slices
salt and pepper

Cut the hare meat, excluding the saddle, into cubes. Mix together the marc, wine, bay leaf and carrots in a dish, add the diced hare, pork blade and diced pork belly and leave to marinate for 24 hours. Preheat the oven to 180°C / 350°F / Gas Mark 4. Drain the marinated meat and chop with the garlic, shallots, savory, rosemary, thyme and parsley. Transfer to a bowl, stir in the cream and season with salt and pepper.

Half-fill a terrine with the meat mixture, place the saddle of hare on top and cover with the remaining meat mixture. Arrange the slices of smoked pork belly on top, overlapping slightly. Put the terrine into a roasting tin (roasting pan), pour in boiling water to come about halfway up the sides and bake for 2 hours. Serve cold.

Veal sweetbreads and smoked ham terrine

Makes 1 kg / 2 ¼ lb
Preparation time: 1 ¾ hours
Cooking time: 2 hours

200 g / 7 oz veal sweetbreads
100 ml / 3 ½ fl oz (scant ½ cup) white wine vinegar
300 g / 11 oz boneless pork throat or hand (arm shoulder), chopped
200 g / 7 oz boneless pork blade (shoulder), chopped
2 shallots, chopped
3 garlic cloves, chopped
100 g / 3 ½ oz (generous ½ cup) smoked lardons
100 ml / 3 ½ fl oz (scant ½ cup) double (heavy) cream
50 ml / 2 fl oz (¼ cup) port
3 fresh flowering thyme sprigs, chopped
pinch of cayenne pepper
6 slices of smoked ham
salt

Put the sweetbreads in a bowl, pour in water to cover, add the vinegar and leave to soak for 1 hour, then drain and rinse well. Put the sweetbreads into a pan, add water to cover and bring to the boil, then lower the heat and simmer for 30 minutes. Drain, remove and discard the skin and cut into 1-cm / ½-inch strips. Preheat the oven to 180°C / 350°F / Gas Mark 4. Mix together the pork throat or hand, pork blade, shallots and garlic in a bowl. Add the lardons, cream, port, thyme and cayenne and season with salt.

Line a terrine with the smoked ham, overlapping the slices. Spoon in half the pork mixture, cover with the sweetbreads and top with the remaining pork mixture. Cover the terrine, put into a roasting tin (roasting pan), pour in boiling water to come about halfway up the sides and bake for 2 hours. Serve cold.

Duck and juniper terrine

Makes 4 x 250-g / 9-oz terrines
Preparation time: 30 minutes
Cooking time: 2 ½ hours

500 g / 1 lb 2 oz boneless duck meat, with skin, cut into cubes
200 g / 7 oz boneless pork blade (shoulder), cut into cubes
200 g / 7 oz boneless pork belly (side), cut into cubes
6 garlic cloves
4 shallots
10 juniper berries
6 fresh tarragon sprigs, finely chopped
1 teaspoon quatre épices
1 teaspoon ground ginger
pinch of piment d'Espelette or other hot dried chilli (chile)
2 eggs, lightly beaten
100 ml / 3 ½ fl oz (scant ½ cup) double (heavy) cream
50 ml / 2 fl oz (¼ cup) Armagnac
salt

Mince (grind) together all the meat and the garlic, shallots and juniper berries
in a bowl. Add the tarragon, spice, ginger and chilli and season with salt. Stir in
the eggs and cream. Rinse out four sterilized preserving jars with Armagnac
and add the remainder to the meat.

Divide the mixture among the jars, taking care avoid any air bubbles.
Seal the jars and immerse them in a pan of water. Put a weight on top to keep
them submerged and bring to the boil. Lower the heat and simmer for 2 ½
hours. These terrines are best eaten two months after they have been cooked.

Duck breast terrine
with green peppercorns

Makes 1 kg / 2¼ lb
Preparation time: 30 minutes
Cooking time: 2 hours

5 tablespoons olive oil
3 onions, chopped
200 g / 7 oz boneless duck meat, chopped
300 g / 11 oz streaky (fatty) bacon, chopped
300 g / 11 oz boneless pork blade (shoulder), chopped
50 ml / 2 fl oz (¼ cup) white port
1 tablespoon green peppercorns
½ teaspoon finely grated orange zest
100 g / 3 ½ oz smoked duck breast, sliced
100 g /3 ½ oz dried duck breast, sliced
salt and pepper

Preheat the oven to 180°C / 350°F / Gas Mark 4. Heat the olive oil in a frying
pan (skillet). Add the onions and cook over a low heat, stirring occasionally,
for 5 minutes, until softened. Remove the pan from the heat. Mix together
the chopped duck meat, bacon and pork blade in a bowl, add the port,
peppercorns, onions and orange zest and season with salt and pepper.

Spoon one-third of the mixture into a terrine and cover with the smoked duck
breast. Spoon in half the remaining mixture and cover with the dried duck
breast. Add the remaining mixture. Cover and bake for 2 hours. Serve cold.

Wild boar terrine with blackcurrants

Makes 1 kg / 2 ¼ lb
Preparation time: 45 minutes
Marinating time: 24 hours
Cooking time: 2 hours

3 onions, chopped
2 garlic cloves, chopped
200 ml / 7 fl oz (scant 1 cup) red wine
finely grated zest of 3 oranges
1 bay leaf
1 tablespoon blackcurrants
400 g / 14 oz boneless shoulder of wild boar, cut into 1-cm / ½-inch cubes
200 g / 7 oz streaky (fatty) bacon
200 g / 7 oz pork blade (shoulder)
50 ml / 2 fl oz (¼ cup) crème de cassis
salt and pepper

Mix together the onions, garlic, wine, orange zest, bay leaf and blackcurrants in a dish. Add the boar and leave to marinate for 24 hours, then drain, reserving the marinade. Preheat the oven to 180°C / 350°F / Gas Mark 4. Coarsely mince (grind) the bacon and pork blade with half the boar, transfer to a bowl and stir in the crème de cassis. Stir the reserved marinade into the mixture. Add the remaining boar and season with salt and pepper.

Spoon the mixture into a terrine, cover and put into a roasting tin (roasting pan). Pour in boiling water to come about halfway up the sides and bake for 2 hours. Serve cold.

Huntsman's terrine

Makes 1 kg / 2 ¼ lb
Preparation time: 45 minutes
Cooking time: 2 hours

2 pigeons (squab), boned, drawn and plucked, hearts and livers reserved
6 tablespoons olive oil
100 ml / 3 ½ fl oz (scant ½ cup) Banyuls or other sweet wine
300 g / 11 oz boneless pork blade (shoulder), chopped
200 g / 7 oz boneless pork belly (side), chopped
2 shallots, chopped
100 g / 3 ½ oz (generous ½ cup) smoked lardons
200 g / 7 oz chanterelle mushrooms
salt and pepper

Chop the pigeon flesh, excluding the breasts. Preheat the oven to 180°C / 350°F / Gas Mark 4. Heat half the olive oil in a frying pan (skillet). Add the hearts and livers and cook, stirring occasionally, for a few minutes. Add the wine and cook, stirring and scraping up the sediment from the base of the pan with a wooden spoon, for a few minutes, then allow to caramelize and remove from the heat. Chop the hearts and livers, transfer to a bowl and add the pork blade, pork belly, chopped pigeon meat and shallots. Stir in the lardons and season with salt and pepper. Heat the remaining olive oil in a frying pan. Add the chanterelles and cook over a low heat, stirring occasionally, for about 8 minutes, until lightly browned.

Make layers of the meat mixture, chanterelles, pigeon breasts, meat mixture, chanterelles, pigeon breasts and meat mixture in a terrine. Cover, put into a roasting tin (roasting pan), pour in boiling water to come about halfway up the sides and bake for 2 hours. Serve cold.

Pressed quail terrine

Makes 1 kg / 2¼ lb
Preparation time: 40 minutes
Cooking time: 1 hour

6 tablespoons olive oil
4 quails, boned with breasts separated
2 tablespoons brandy
3 garlic cloves
6 fresh parsley sprigs
200 g / 7 oz porcini mushrooms, thawed if frozen
400 g / 14 oz skinless, boneless chicken breasts, chopped
5 eggs
250 ml / 8 fl oz (1 cup) double (heavy) cream
pinch of grated nutmeg
pinch of piment d'Espelette or other hot dried chilli (chile)
salt and pepper

Preheat the oven to 180°C / 350°F / Gas Mark 4. Heat half the olive oil in
a frying pan (skillet). Add the quail breast fillets and cook over a high heat for
5–8 minutes, until browned. Pour in the brandy, heat for a few seconds and
ignite. When the flames have died down, remove the pan from the heat. Chop
the garlic with the parsley. Heat the remaining oil in a pan. Add the porcini and
cook over a medium-low heat, stirring occasionally, for 5 minutes, until they
have given off their liquid. Stir in the garlic and parsley mixture and cook,
stirring occasionally, until the porcini are lightly browned. Put the chicken,
eggs, cream, nutmeg, chilli and the quail leg meat into a food processor or
blender and process until smooth and thoroughly combined. Transfer to a bowl
and season with salt and pepper.

Make layers of chicken mixture, porcini, quail breasts, chicken mixture, porcini,
quail breasts and chicken mixture in a terrine. Cover, put the terrine into a
roasting tin (roasting pan), pour in water to come about halfway up the sides
and bake for 1 hour. Serve cold.

Shoulder of lamb terrine

Makes 1 kg / 2 ¼ lb
Preparation time: 5 ½ hours
Standing time: 24 hours

120 ml / 4 fl oz (½ cup) olive oil
1 shoulder of lamb
3 garlic cloves
2 onions
500 ml / 18 fl oz (2 ¼ cups) slightly sweet Jurançon
   or other dry white wine
3 calf's feet
3 fresh thyme sprigs
1 fresh rosemary sprig
1 teaspoon ground cumin
1 bunch of fresh mint
salt and pepper

Preheat the oven to 120°C / 250°F / Gas Mark ½. Heat the olive oil in a flameproof casserole. Add the shoulder of lamb and cook over a medium heat, turning frequently, for about 10 minutes, until lightly browned all over. Lower the heat, add the garlic cloves and onions and cook, stirring occasionally, for about 10 minutes, until browned. Pour in half the wine and 250 ml / 8 fl oz (1 cup) water, add the calf's feet, thyme, rosemary, cumin and half the mint. Cover, transfer to the oven and cook, basting occasionally and gradually adding the remaining wine and another 250 ml / 8 fl oz (1 cup) water, for 5 hours, until the meat comes away from the bone and about 200 ml / 7 fl oz (scant 1 cup) of the cooking liquid remains.

Lift out the lamb shoulder and calf's feet. Cut the lamb off the bones, remove the meat from the calf's feet, chop the remaining mint and mix together in a bowl. Season with salt and pepper. Fill a terrine with the meat without pressing down too much and strain in the cooking liquid to cover completely. Cover and leave to stand in a cool place for 24 hours.

Our bistro cook, Guy, is passionate about quality. He uses only the finest ingredients to make good, honest food that is guaranteed to appeal to everyone.

Guy's Foie gras with quinces

Makes 1 kg / 2 ¼ lb
Preparation time: 70 minutes
Standing time: 24 hours

4 quinces, peeled, cored and quartered
1 kg / 2 ¼ lb (5 cups) caster (superfine) sugar
1 kg / 2 ¼ lb fresh or frozen foie gras, cut into 2-cm / ¾-inch slices
salt and pepper

Thinly slice the quinces. Put the sugar into a pan, stir in 500 ml / 18 fl oz (2 ¼ cups) water and heat gently, stirring constantly, until the sugar has dissolved. Bring to the boil and cook until golden brown in colour. Stir in more water to give the caramel a liquid consistency. Add the quinces to the caramel and simmer for 40 minutes, until they are tender but not disintegrating. Heat a non-stick pan. Add the foie gras and cook until the slices are light golden brown on both sides but still firm. Remove from the heat and season with salt and pepper.

Fill a terrine while the ingredients are still hot. Make alternating layers of foie gras and quinces. Press down lightly, cover the terrine with cling film (plastic wrap) and chill in the refrigerator for 24 hours before serving.

Etienne has been running a bistro in Saint-Cloud for 10 years, and his terrines are his signature dishes. Being such a popular choice, it's lucky that they are easily shared amongst everyone!

Etienne's Pig's cheeks

Makes 1 kg / 2 ¼ lb
Preparation time: 4 hours
Standing time: 24 hours

6 tablespoons olive oil
1 kg / 2 ¼ lb pig's cheeks
3 shallots, chopped
4 garlic cloves, crushed
3 carrots, cut into 1-cm / ½-inch lengths
500 ml / 18 fl oz (2 ¼ cups) white wine
4 calf's feet
1 large fresh parsley sprig, coarsely chopped
salt and pepper

Heat the olive oil in a large pan. Add the pig's cheeks and cook over a medium heat, turning occasionally, for 8–10 minutes, until lightly browned. Add the shallots, garlic cloves and carrots and cook, stirring occasionally, for 4–5 minutes, until softened. Pour in the white wine, add the calf's feet and pour in water to cover – about twice the volume of the meat. Cook over a low heat for 3 hours, until the pig's cheeks are very tender. Lift out the meat and vegetables from the pan. Cut off the meat from the calf's feet and chop the pig's cheeks. Mix all the ingredients together in a bowl and season with salt and pepper.

Spoon the mixture into a terrine without pressing down. Bring the cooking liquid back to the boil and cook until reduced to 300 ml / ½ pint (1 ¼ cups). Pour it into the terrine to cover the meat completely. Chill in the refrigerator for 24 hours before serving.

SAUCES & GARNISHES
for the meat terrines

Pickled vegetables

1 courgette (zucchini)
10 cherry tomatoes
5 spring onions (scallions), trimmed and halved
3 carrots, halved lengthways
1 fresh tarragon sprig
1 bay leaf
300 ml / ½ pint (1 ¼ cups) white wine vinegar

Cut the courgette into quarters and remove the core.
Put all the vegetables in a sterilized preserving jar
and place the tarragon sprig and bay leaf in the
middle. Pour in the vinegar to cover and seal tightly.
Store in a cool place for two weeks before eating.

Porcini in olive oil

400 g / 14 oz porcini
1 fresh thyme sprig
1 fresh rosemary sprig
1 bay leaf
2 garlic cloves
300 ml / ½ pint (1 ¼ cups) olive oil
salt and pepper

Blanch the porcini in boiling water for 10 seconds,
then drain. Pack them into a jar and add the thyme,
rosemary, bay leaf and garlic cloves. Season the
olive oil with salt and pepper and pour it into the jar
to cover the porcini.

Mango chutney

2 onions, finely diced
2 mangoes, peeled and finely diced
100 g / 3 ½ oz (½ cup) brown sugar
100 ml / 3 ½ fl oz (scant ½ cup) balsamic vinegar

Put the onions and mangoes into a pan, add the
sugar and pour in the vinegar. Cook over a medium
heat, stirring until the sugar has dissolved. Lower
the heat and simmer, stirring occasionally, for about
2 hours, until shiny and caramelized.

Onion marmalade

6 tablespoons olive oil
4 onions, thinly sliced
3 tablespoons brown sugar
1 tablespoon grenadine
100 ml / 3 ½ fl oz (scant ½ cup) white wine
salt and pepper

Heat the olive oil in a pan. Add the onions and cook
over a very low heat, stirring occasionally, for 10–15
minutes, until browned. Stir in the brown sugar and
grenadine and cook until caramelized, then pour in
the wine and 300 ml / ½ pint (1 ¼ cups) water.
Simmer very gently until syrupy, then season with
salt and pepper.

CHEESE

Cheese terrines provide an interesting alternative to traditional meat pâtés, and also add a creative and personal touch to your cheeseboard. Combining cheeses with vegetables, fruit, herbs and nuts in a terrine creates a wonderful and often surprising mix of tastes and textures.

Gorgonzola, mascarpone and nut terrine

Serves 6–8
Preparation time: 30 minutes
Standing time: 1 hour

150 g / 5 oz mascarpone cheese
3 tablespoons hazelnuts
3 tablespoons pistachio nuts
1 ½ tablespoons chopped dried apricots
½ teaspoon coarsely ground black pepper
1 teaspoon clear honey
300 g / 11 oz mature Gorgonzola cheese, rind removed

Mash the mascarpone with a fork in a bowl. Add the nuts, apricots, pepper and honey and mix well. Line a rectangular terrine with cling film (plastic wrap), allowing it to overhang the sides. Cut the Gorgonzola into slices about one-third the depth of the terrine.

Make a layer of Gorgonzola in the terrine, spoon in the mascarpone mixture and top with another layer of Gorgonzola. Wrap the overhanging cling film over the top to seal and leave to stand in a cool place for 1 hour. Turn out and remove the cling film before serving.

Pear and Fourme d'Ambert terrine

Serves 6
Preparation time: 30 minutes
Standing time: 1 hour

20 g / ¾ oz (1 ½ tablespoons) unsalted butter
(sweet butter)
1 pear, peeled, cored and quartered
1 teaspoon brown sugar
200 g / 7 oz mature Fourme d'Ambert
or other blue cheese
2 tablespoons ruby port
20 g / ¾ oz (1 ½ tablespoons) slightly salted butter

Melt the unsalted butter in a pan. Add the pears
and sugar and cook, stirring occasionally, until
caramelized, then remove from the heat. Mix the
Fourme d'Ambert with the port and slightly salted
butter in a bowl. Line a terrine with cling film
(plastic wrap), allowing it to overhang the sides, and
make alternating layers of the cheese mixture and
pear mixture, ending with a layer of cheese mixture.
Wrap the overhanging cling film over the top to seal
and leave to stand in a cool place for 1 hour. Turn
out and remove the cling film before serving.

Sainte-Maure, basil and fresh herb terrine

Serves 4
Preparation time: 20 minutes

100 g / 3 ½ oz (7 tablespoons) slightly salted butter,
softened
½ shallot, finely chopped
4 fresh chives, finely chopped
1 tablespoon walnut oil
½ teaspoon coarsely ground black pepper
1 fresh Sainte-Maure or other goats' cheese
4 fresh basil leaves
sea salt

Mix together the butter, shallot, chives, walnut oil
and pepper in a bowl. Cut the cheese into four thick
slices. Divide the shallot butter and basil leaves
among the slices and reassemble the cheese.
Sprinkle with sea salt.

Tomato confit and mozzarella terrine

Serves 6
Preparation time: 20 minutes
Standing time: 3 hours

3 large tomatoes
6 fresh basil sprigs
200 g / 7 oz mozzarella cheese, thinly sliced
olive oil, for drizzling
sea salt

Make a cross in the tops of the tomatoes and cut out the stems. Bring a pan of water to the boil, plunge in the tomatoes for a few seconds, remove and refresh in iced water. Skin the tomatoes and cut them into strips, discarding the cores. Put the tomato strips on a sheet of greaseproof (waxed) paper and sprinkle with sea salt. Leave in a cool place for 1 hour, then pat dry to remove the excess salt. Strip the leaves from the basil. Fill a round terrine with layers of tomatoes, basil and mozzarella, drizzling with olive oil at regular intervals, then press down. Chill in the refrigerator for 2 hours before serving.

Brousse de Brebis terrine

Serves 4
Preparation time: 20 minutes

1 courgette (zucchini), about 250 g / 9 oz
100 g / 3 ½ oz Brousse de Brebis or other ewes' milk curd cheese (soft sheep cheese)
1–2 teaspoons piment d'Espelette or other hot dried chilli (chile)
3 fresh chives, finely chopped
salt

Using a mandoline or sharp knife, cut the courgettes lengthways into thin slices (cut the first one a little thicker and then discard it in order to create a stable base). Mash the Brousse de Brebis with a fork in a bowl, stir in the chilli and chives to taste and season with salt. Reassemble the courgette by inserting a thin layer of the cheese mixture between each slice. Smooth the sides with a spatula.

Roquefort and pain d'épice terrine

Serves 6
Preparation time: 20 minutes
Standing time: 1 hour

3 slices of pain d'épice or other gingerbread, cut lengthways
200 g / 7 oz Roquefort cheese
100 g / 3 ½ oz (7 tablespoons) butter, softened
1 celery stick (stalk), diced

Preheat the grill (broiler). Put the slices of gingerbread on the grill rack and grill until lightly toasted on both sides. Remove from the heat. Mash the Roquefort in a bowl with a fork and stir in the butter and celery. Spread a layer of the Roquefort mixture on two slices of gingerbread to the same thickness as the slices themselves. Sandwich the two spread slices together and top with the third slice. Smooth the sides with a spatula. Wrap in cling film (plastic wrap) and leave to stand in a cool place for 1 hour. Remove the cling film before serving.

If you would like to make your own pain d'épice, you can do so as follows:

400 ml / 14 fl oz (1 ¾ cups) warm water
400 ml / 14 fl oz (1 ¾ cups) honey
150 g / 5 oz (⅔ cup) sugar
50 ml / 2 fl oz (¼ cup) rum
150 g / 5 oz (1 ¼ cups) rye flour
200 g / 7 oz (1 ¾ cups) plain (all-purpose) flour
100 g / 3 ½ oz (scant 1 cup) buckwheat flour
100 g / 3 ½ oz (scant ½ cup) crystallized (candied) fruit
zest of 1 lemon

zest of 1 orange
pinch of ground cinnamon
pinch of fine salt
pinch of grated nutmeg
50 ml / 2 fl oz (¼ cup) Pernod
120 g / 4 oz (½ cup) currants
70 g / 2 ¾ oz (scant ¾ cup) flaked (sliced) almonds
3 tablespoons bicarbonate of soda (baking soda)

Mix together the water, honey, sugar and rum in a bowl. Put all of the flours into another bowl, add the honey mixture and stir until smooth and thoroughly combined. Finely dice the crystallized fruit, and add it to the bowl along with the lemon and orange zest, cinnamon, salt, nutmeg, Pernod, currants, almonds and soda and mix well. Cover with cling film (plastic wrap) and chill in the refrigerator for 48 hours. Preheat the oven to 180°C / 350°F / Gas Mark 4. Line a loaf pan with greaseproof (waxed) paper, allowing it to overhang the sides slightly. Spoon the mixture into the pan, and bake for 1 hour. Leave to cool completely, then remove from the pan and discard the greaseproof paper before serving.

Camembert, apple and multigrain bread terrine

Serves 4
Preparation time: 20 minutes

1 mature (sharp) Camembert cheese
4 tablespoons olive oil
2 slices of multigrain bread, cut into cubes
½ Granny Smith or other tart green apple
juice of ½ lemon

Take the Camembert out of the refrigerator just before preparation and at least 1 hour before serving. Heat the olive oil in a frying pan (skillet). Add the cubes of bread and cook, stirring and tossing frequently, for a few minutes, until golden brown all over. Remove with a slotted spoon and drain on a paper towel.

Core the apple, cut it into cubes the same size as the bread and drizzle with the lemon juice. Trim the sides of the cheese and halve it horizontally. Line the two inner sides of the Camembert with the croûtons and apple cubes and stack them. Leave to stand in a cool place before serving.

SAUCES
for the cheese terrines

Preserves

(for Comté, Gruyère, Brebis, etc.)

Surprise your guests by offering different preserves, from black cherry to bitter orange, as garnishes for cheese. It's down to you to find good combinations.

Walnut oil with shallots

(for mild cheeses)

2 shallots, chopped
1 bunch of fresh chives, chopped
150 ml / ¼ pint (⅔ cup) walnut oil
100 ml / 3 ⅛ fl oz (scant ½ cup) sunflower oil
salt and pepper

Mix together the shallots, chives and two oils in a bowl and season with salt and pepper.

Walnut and celery cream

(for parsley-flavoured pâtés)

1 celery stick (stalk) with leaves
3 tablespoons double (heavy) cream
1 tablespoon walnut oil
100 g / 3 ½ oz (scant 1 cup) walnuts
salt and pepper

Thinly slice the celery stick and cut two celery leaves into thin julienne strips. Mix together the cream and walnut oil in a bowl and add the walnuts and celery slices. Season well with salt and pepper and sprinkle with the celery leaves.

Honey and nut sauce

(for Camembert, Brie, etc.)

1 teaspoon hazelnuts, coarsely crushed
1 teaspoon pistachio nuts, coarsely crushed
1 teaspoon almonds, coarsely crushed
3 stoned (pitted) prunes, finely chopped
3 dried apricots, finely chopped
2 tablespoons chestnut honey
coarsely ground black pepper

Mix together the hazelnuts, pistachios, almonds, prunes and apricots in a bowl. Stir in the honey and season with a little coarsely ground black pepper.

DESSERTS

Terrines shouldn't be kept for only the first courses of your menu.
They can also be a perfect solution for those with a sweet tooth. With their
multi-layered construction and silky or rugged textures, chocolate, fruit
or nut terrines are a spectacular conclusion to a fabulous meal.

Tropical fruit terrine

Serves 6
Preparation time: 30 minutes
Standing time: 4 hours

150 g / 5 oz peaches, peeled and stoned (pitted)
150 g / 5 oz pineapple, peeled
150 g / 5 oz papaya, peeled and seeded
150 g / 5 oz mango, peeled and stoned (pitted)
juice of 1 lemon
150 g / 5 oz (scant 1 cup) raspberries
150 g / 5 oz (1 ¼ cups) strawberries, halved
4 gelatine (gelatin) leaves
150 ml / ¼ pint (⅔ cup) pineapple juice
150 ml / ¼ pint (⅔ cup) apple juice
50 ml / 2 fl oz (½ cup) pear schnapps (eau-de-vie)
100 g / 3 ½ oz (¼ cup) sugar
3 passion fruits
2 kiwis, sliced

Cut the peaches, pineapple, papaya and mango into the same size cubes
and mix with the lemon juice in a bowl. Add the raspberries and strawberries.
Pour a little water into a small bowl, add the gelatine and leave to soften for
5 minutes. Mix together the pineapple juice, apple juice and pear schnapps in
a pan and stir in the sugar. Halve the passion fruits, scoop out the pulp, strain
to remove the seeds if you like, and add to the pan with the kiwis. Bring
the juice mixture to the boil. Squeeze out the gelatine and add it to the pan,
whisking constantly, then remove the pan from the heat.

Line a terrine with cling film (plastic wrap), allowing it to overhang the sides.
Arrange the fruit in the terrine and pour in the juice mixture to cover. Wrap
the overhanging cling film over the top to seal and chill in the refrigerator for
4 hours. Turn out and remove the cling film before serving.

Citrus fruit terrine

Serves 4
Preparation time: 45 minutes
Standing time: 3 hours

8 oranges
3 pomelos (if unavailable, substitute ruby red grapefruit)
4 gelatine (gelatin) leaves
juice of 1 lemon
150 g / 5 oz (⅔ cup) brown sugar
50 ml / 2 fl oz (¼ cup) Cointreau
pinch of ground cinnamon

Working over a bowl to catch the juice, cut off the skin and bitter white pith from the oranges and pomelos, then cut the flesh into quarters. Line a terrine with cling film (plastic wrap), allowing it to overhang the sides, and make alternating layers of the orange and pomelo quarters. Pour a little water into a small bowl, add the gelatine and leave to soften for 5 minutes. Pour the lemon juice and any juice from the oranges and pomelos into a pan and bring to the boil, then stir in the brown sugar, Cointreau and cinnamon. Squeeze out the gelatine and add to the liquid, whisking constantly. Pour the juice mixture into the terrine to cover and wrap the overhanging cling film over the top to seal. Chill in the refrigerator for 3 hours, until set. Turn out and remove the cling film before serving.

Tarte tatin terrine

Serves 6
Preparation time: 30 minutes
Cooking time: 2 hours

10 Granny Smith or other tart green apples
100 g / 3 ½ oz (7 tablespoons) butter
1 teaspoon ground cinnamon
1 teaspoon grated fresh root ginger
150 g / 5 oz (⅔ cup) muscovado (molasses) sugar
100 g / 3 ½ oz (scant 1 cup) slivered almonds

Preheat the oven to 180°C / 350°F / Gas Mark 4. Peel, core, halve and thinly slice the apples. Melt the butter in a frying pan (skillet) and stir in the cinnamon, ginger and sugar, then remove from the heat. Brush a terrine with the melted butter mixture and make a layer of apples. Make a layer of almonds and add more of the melted butter mixture. Repeat the layers until the terrine is full and all the ingredients have been used up. Cover the terrine, put it into a roasting tin (roasting pan), pour in boiling water to come about halfway up the sides and bake for 2 hours. Serve warm after carefully removing from the terrine. Alternatively, serve straight from the dish.

Apple in Calvados terrine

Serves 6
Preparation time: 30 minutes
Standing time: 4 hours

1 litre / 1 ¾ pints (4 cups) apple juice
pinch of ground cinnamon
pinch of grated nutmeg
6 Granny Smith or other tart green apples
50 g / 2 oz (¼ cup) butter
100 g / 3 ½ oz (scant ½ cup) muscovado (molasses) sugar
1 tablespoon clear honey
100 ml / 3 ½ fl oz (scant ½ cup) Calvados
3 gelatine (gelatin) leaves

Pour the apple juice into a pan, add the cinnamon and nutmeg and bring to the boil. Cook until the liquid has reduced to two-thirds, then remove the pan from the heat. Peel and core the apples, then cut them into large cubes. Melt the butter in a frying pan (skillet), add the apples, sugar and honey and cook, stirring, until caramelized. Pour in the Calvados, heat for a few seconds and ignite. When the flames have died down, remove the pan from the heat. Pour a little water into a small bowl, add the gelatine and leave to soften for 5 minutes. Squeeze out the gelatine and add to the warm reduced juice, whisking constantly. Line a terrine with cling film (plastic wrap), allowing it to overhang the sides, then fill with the caramelized apples and pour in the juice to cover. Wrap the overhanging cling film over the top to seal and leave in a cool place for 4 hours. Turn out and remove the cling film before serving.

Strawberry and fresh mint terrine

Serves 6
Preparation time: 30 minutes
Standing time: 12 hours

600 g / 1 lb 5 oz (5 ¼ cups) strawberries
4 gelatine (gelatin) leaves
3 oranges
juice of 1 pomelo (if unavailable, substitute
    ruby red grapefruit)
100 g / 3 ½ oz (scant ½ cup) brown sugar
pinch of Sichuan pepper
½ teaspoon grated fresh root ginger
4 fresh mint sprigs, finely chopped

Rinse the strawberries and dry gently with a cloth, then hull and halve lengthways. Line a terrine with cling film (plastic wrap), allowing it to overhang the sides. Fill with the strawberries, placing the cut sides against the cling film, without pressing down. Pour a little water into a small bowl, add the gelatine and leave to soften for 5 minutes. Grate the zest of one orange. Squeeze the juice from all the oranges and pour into a pan. Add the pomelo juice, sugar, pepper, ginger and orange zest and bring to the boil. Squeeze out the gelatine and add to the juice, whisking constantly. Remove from the heat and add the mint. Pour the juice into the terrine to cover. Wrap the overhanging cling film over the top to seal and leave to stand in a cool place for 12 hours. Turn out and remove the cling film before serving.

Chocolate and raspberry terrine

Serves 6
Preparation time: 1 hour
Standing time: 1 hour

300 g / 11 oz (scant 2 cups) raspberries

For the feuillantine:
100 g / 3 ½ oz milk chocolate, broken into pieces
200 g /7 oz praline paste
100 g / 3 ½ oz feuilletine, gaufrette or other sweet wafers, crushed

For the chocolate cream:
100 ml / 3 ½ fl oz (scant ½ cup) double (heavy) cream
100 g / 3 ½ oz dark (bittersweet) chocolate, broken into pieces
100 g / 3 ½ oz hazelnut and chocolate spread

Line a rectangular tray with greaseproof (waxed) paper. To make the feuillantine, melt the chocolate with the praline paste in a heatproof bowl set over a pan of barely simmering water. Remove from the heat and stir in the crushed wafers. Spoon the mixture onto the prepared tray, place a sheet of greaseproof paper on top and spread the feuillantine with a rolling pin to make a thin rectangle. Chill in the freezer for 20 minutes. Meanwhile, make the chocolate cream. Pour the cream into a pan and bring to the boil. Remove the pan from the heat and stir in the dark chocolate and the hazelnut and chocolate spread until melted and smooth. Leave to cool at room temperature.

Cut four rectangles of feuillantine, spread a strip of chocolate cream along the centre of two of them and place raspberries all around and along the entire length. Reverse the process (raspberries–chocolate) on a third rectangle. Stack all the rectangles as shown. Leave to stand in a cool place for 1 hour before serving.

Milk chocolate crêpe terrine

Serves 6
Preparation time: 20 minutes
Cooking time: 1 hour

For the crêpe batter:
3 eggs
1 sachet vanilla sugar
300 g / 11 oz (2 ¾ cups) plain (all-purpose) flour
400 ml / 14 fl oz (1 ¾ cups) milk
25 g / 1 oz (2 tablespoons) butter, melted
1 tablespoon sunflower oil

For the chocolate sauce:
200 g / 7 oz milk chocolate, broken into pieces
100 ml / 3 ½ fl oz (scant ½ cups) double (heavy) cream
20 g / ¾ oz (1 ½ tablespoons) butter
pinch of ground cinnamon
pinch of ground ginger

To make the batter, beat the eggs well, then add the vanilla sugar and flour. Gradually stir in the milk and 200 ml / 7 fl oz (scant 1 cup) water. Finally, stir in the melted butter and the sunflower oil. To make the chocolate sauce, put the chocolate, cream, butter, cinnamon and ginger into a heatproof bowl set over a pan of barely simmering water. Heat, stirring occasionally, until the chocolate has melted and the mixture has blended together. Keep warm.

Cook the crêpes in a non-stick pan (skillet), making sure that they are very thin. Set aside in a warm place. When they are all cooked, brush them with the chocolate mixture and stack them on top of each other. Serve warm.

All chocolate terrine

Serves 8
Preparation time: 35 minutes
Standing time: 24 hours

400 g / 14 oz dark (bittersweet) chocolate, broken
    into pieces
125 g / 4 ¼ oz (generous ½ cup) butter
75 g / 2 ¾ oz (⅔ cup) icing (confectioner's) sugar
4 egg yolks
500 ml / 18 fl oz (2 ¼ cups) double (heavy) cream

Melt the chocolate with the butter in a heatproof bowl set
over a pan of barely simmering water. Whisk in the icing
sugar and egg yolks, then leave to cool, stirring frequently.
Meanwhile, stiffly whisk the cream in another bowl. When
the chocolate mixture is no longer hot to the touch, gently
fold in the cream with a flexible spatula. Line a terrine with
cling film (plastic wrap), allowing it to overhang the sides
generously. Spoon in the chocolate mixture, pressing down
well. Wrap the overhanging cling film over the top to seal
and chill in the refrigerator for 24 hours. Turn out and
remove the cling film before serving.

Frozen nougat and prune terrine

Serves 6
Preparation time: 30 minutes
Freezing time: 24 hours

sunflower oil, for brushing
250 g / 9 oz (1 ¼ cups) sugar
150 g / 5 oz (1 ¼ cups) slivered almonds
500 ml / 18 fl oz (2 ¼ cups) double (heavy) cream
8 egg whites
200 g / 7 oz (scant 1 cup) stoned (pitted) prunes,
    coarsely chopped

Brush a sheet of greaseproof (waxed) paper with sunflower
oil. Heat the sugar in a dry pan until it melts, then boil it
until it is caramelized and light brown. Stir in the almonds
and pour the mixture onto the greaseproof paper. Leave to
cool completely, then chop coarsely. Stiffly whisk the
cream. Stiffly whisk the egg whites in a grease-free bowl,
then gently fold them into the cream with a flexible spatula.
Fold in the prunes and nougatine. Line a terrine with
greaseproof paper, spoon in the mixture and freeze for
24 hours. Turn out and remove the greaseproof paper
before serving.

Chocolate and glacé cherry terrine

Serves 6
Preparation time: 45 minutes
Standing time: 12 hours

250 g / 9 oz dark (bittersweet) chocolate,
    broken into pieces
150 g / 5 oz (⅔ cup) butter
4 eggs, separated
100 g / 3 ½ oz (½ cup) sugar
100 ml / 3 ½ oz (scant ½ cup) double (heavy) cream
100 g / 3 ½ oz (scant ½ cup) mascarpone cheese
100 g / 3 ½ oz amarena cherries (if unavailable, substitute
    morello cherries)
salt

Melt the chocolate with the butter in a heatproof bowl set
over a pan of barely simmering water, then remove from the
heat. Beat the egg yolks with the sugar until pale in colour.
Stiffly whisk the egg whites with a pinch of salt in a
grease-free bowl. Mix together the egg yolk mixture and
chocolate mixture, then gently fold in the egg whites.
Stiffly whisk the cream in another bowl and fold it into the
mascarpone. Pipe a layer of the chocolate mixture into
individual round dishes and divide the cherries among
them. Cover with the cream and mascarpone mixture and
top with another layer of chocolate. Leave to stand in
a cool place for 12 hours.

Coffee terrine

Serves 6
Preparation time: 30 minutes
Standing time: 24 hours

6 egg yolks
200 g / 7 oz (1 cup) caster (superfine) sugar
6 gelatine (gelatin) leaves
800 ml / 1 pint 8 fl oz (3 ½ cups) milk
3 tablespoons chicory extract
200 ml / 7 fl oz (scant 1 cup) double (heavy) cream
12 sponge fingers (ladyfingers)
150 ml / ¼ pint (⅔ cup) freshly brewed coffee

Beat the egg yolks with the sugar until pale in colour. Pour a little water into
a small bowl, add the gelatine and leave to soften for 5 minutes. Pour the milk
into a pan, bring to the boil and pour it into the egg yolk mixture, whisking
constantly. Squeeze out the gelatine and add it to the milk and egg yolk mixture
with the chicory extract. Pour this mixture into a pan and cook over a very low
heat, stirring constantly, until it thickens enough to coat the back of the spoon.
Remove the pan from the heat and leave to cool, whisking frequently. Stiffly
whisk the cream and gently fold it into the cooled chicory mixture. Soak
three-quarters of the sponge fingers in the coffee.

Line a terrine with cling film (plastic wrap), allowing it to overhang the sides,
and add the coffee-soaked biscuits. Cover with the chicory mixture and top
with a layer of dry biscuits. Wrap the overhanging cling film over the top to
seal and chill in the refrigerator for 24 hours. Turn out and remove the cling
film before serving.

Cheesecake terrine

Serves 6
Preparation time: 1 hour
Standing time: 1 hour

For the cake
4 eggs, separated
200 g / 7 oz (1 cup) caster (superfine) sugar
150 g / 5 oz (1 ¼ cups) plain (all-purpose) flour, sifted
2 teaspoons baking powder
2 tablespoons lemon juice
2 tablespoons rum
200 g / 7 oz (scant 1 ½ cups) carrots, grated
150 g / 5 oz (1 ¼ cups) almonds, chopped
grated zest of 1 orange
250 ml / 8 fl oz (1 cup) orange juice

For the filling
150 g / 5 oz (⅔ cup) mascarpone cheese
100 g / 3 ½ oz (½ cup) muscovado (molasses) sugar
1 teaspoon ground cinnamon
100 g / 3 ½ oz (scant ½ cup) curd (farmer's) cheese, beaten

Preheat the oven to 160°C / 325°F / Gas Mark 3. To make the cake, beat the
egg yolks with the sugar until pale in colour. Sift in the flour and baking
powder, add the lemon juice, rum, carrots, almonds and orange zest and mix
well. Stiffly whisk the egg whites in a grease-free bowl and gently fold in
with a flexible spatula.

Line a terrine with greaseproof (waxed) paper and spoon in the cake mixture
until two-thirds full. Bake for 40 minutes, then remove from the oven and turn
out onto a wire rack to cool. Cut the cake in half horizontally and sprinkle
with the orange juice. Mix all the filling ingredients together in a bowl. Line the
terrine with cling film (plastic wrap), allowing it to overhang the sides, put half
the cake in it, cover with the filling and top with the other half of the cake. Wrap
the overhanging cling film over the top to seal, and chill in the refrigerator for
1 hour. Turn out and remove the cling film before serving.

Chestnut, meringue and chantilly terrine

Serves 6
Preparation time: 20 minutes
Cooking time: 2 hours (for the meringues)

For the meringues
4 egg whites
100 g / 3 ½ oz (½ cup) caster (superfine) sugar
100 g / 3 ½ oz (scant 1 cup) icing (confectioner's) sugar

300 ml / ½ pint (1 ¼ cups) double (heavy) cream
200 g / 7 oz chestnut purée
50 g / 2 oz marrons glacés, broken into pieces

Preheat the oven to 110°C / 225°F / Gas Mark ¼. Line one or two baking sheets (cookie sheets) with greaseproof (waxed) paper. To make the meringues, stiffly whisk the egg whites with the caster sugar in a grease-free bowl. Gently fold in the icing sugar with a flexible spatula. Spoon the mixture into an icing bag and pipe three even rounds onto the prepared baking sheets. Bake for 2 hours without opening the oven door. Remove from the oven and leave to cool.

Stiffly whisk the cream. Coat a meringue round with half the chestnut purée, add half the pieces of marron glacé and cover with half the cream. Place another meringue round on top and cover with the remaining chestnut purée, marron glacé and cream in the same way. Top with the final meringue round. You can make individual terrines with smaller meringue rounds, if you like.

Diplomat pudding

Serves 6–8
Preparation time: 20 minutes
Cooking time: 30 minutes

500 ml / 18 fl oz (2 ¼ cups) milk
100 ml / 3 ½ fl oz (scant ½ cup) double (heavy) cream
1 vanilla pod (bean)
3 eggs
2 egg yolks
200 g / 7 oz (1 cup) caster (superfine) sugar
300 g / 11 oz sponge fingers (ladyfingers)
100 g / 3 ½ oz (½ cup) crystallized (candied) fruit

Preheat the oven to 180°C / 350°F / Gas Mark 4. Pour the milk and cream into a bowl. Slit the vanilla pod lengthways, scrape out the flesh and seeds into the bowl and mix well. Whisk together the eggs and egg yolks, then whisk them into the milk mixture with the sugar. Line a terrine with cling film (plastic wrap), allowing it to overhang the sides generously.

Make a layer of sponge fingers on the base of the terrine and pour in a quarter of the egg and milk mixture. When the biscuits have soaked up the liquid, sprinkle with crystallized fruit. Continue making layers in this way until the terrine is full and the ingredients have been used up. Wrap the overhanging cling film over the top to seal. Put the terrine into a roasting tin (roasting pan), pour in boiling water to come about halfway up the sides and bake for 30 minutes. Allow to cool completely, then turn out and remove the cling film before serving. Serve cold.

Philippe's bakery in Lyon is famous for the delicious pralines he makes there – when you find them hidden in the middle of a terrine like this, it gives the most irresistible crunchy surprise.

Philippe's Praline terrine

Serves 6
Preparation time: 20 minutes
Cooking time: 45 minutes

125 g / 4 ¼ oz (generous ½ cup) butter
100 g / 3 ½ oz (½ cup) caster (superfine) sugar
150 g / 5 oz (1 ¼ cups) plain (all-purpose) flour
1 teaspoon baking powder
3 eggs lightly beaten
65 g / 2 ½ oz praline, crushed
salt

Preheat the oven to 160°C / 325°F / Gas Mark 3. Beat the butter with the sugar until pale in colour. Sift in the flour, baking powder and a small pinch of salt and mix well. Finally, stir in the eggs and praline.

Line a terrine with greaseproof (waxed) paper, spoon in the mixture and bake for 45 minutes. Allow to cool completely, then turn out and remove the greaseproof paper before serving. Serve cold.

SAUCES
for the sweet terrines

Crème anglaise

8 egg yolks
200 g / 7 oz (1 cup) sugar
600 ml / 1 pint (2 ½ cups) milk
200 ml / 7 fl oz (scant 1 cup) double (heavy) cream
1 vanilla pod (bean)

Beat the egg yolks with the sugar until pale in colour.
Pour the milk and cream into a pan. Slit the vanilla
pod lengthways and scrape out the flesh and seeds
into the pan. Bring the milk and cream mixture to
the boil, then remove the pan from the heat and pour
the liquid into the egg yolk mixture, stirring
constantly. Transfer to a clean pan and cook over
a very low heat, stirring constantly, until the mixture
thickens enough to coat the back of the spoon.

Chocolate and cinnamon

200 ml / 7 fl oz (scant 1 cup) double (heavy) cream
100 g / 3 ½ oz milk chocolate, broken into pieces
1 tablespoon mascarpone cheese
1 teaspoon caster (superfine) sugar
pinch of ground cinnamon

Pour the cream into a pan and bring to the boil. Remove
the pan from the heat, add the chocolate and stir until
melted. (If it is necessary to reheat this sauce, do so in
a heatproof bowl set over a pan of barely simmering
water.) Whisk the mascarpone with the sugar and
cinnamon. Serve the chocolate sauce topped with the
cinnamon-flavoured mascarpone.

Caramel sauce

200 g / 7 oz (1 cup) caster (superfine) sugar
65 g / 2 ½ oz (5 tablespoons) slightly salted butter,
   diced
250 ml / 8 fl oz (1 cup) double (heavy) cream

Pour 100 ml / 3 ½ fl oz (scant ½ cup) water into
a pan, add the sugar and heat gently, stirring
constantly, until the mixture turns a clear golden
colour. Stir in the butter and cream and cook until the
sauce has the desired consistency. (The cooking time
depends on the type of caramel required.)

Fruit coulis

200 g /7 oz seasonal fruit
50 g /2 oz (¼ cup) caster (superfine) sugar
1 tablespoon orange flower water

Put the fruit in a pan, add the sugar and orange flower
water, pour in 200 ml / 7 fl oz (scant 1 cup) water and
cook over a low heat, until softened. Transfer to a food
processor or blender and process until smooth, then
strain and chill in the refrigerator.

INDEX

&

a glossary of terms and ingredients

Index

Glossary

Armagnac
A fine French brandy from the Armagnac region, aged in oak for up to 40 years.

Bouquet garni
Bunches of various combinations of herbs added during cooking and removed before serving. A classic bouquet garni is 3 sprigs fresh parsley, 1 sprig fresh thyme and 1 bay leaf. Herbs are tied together or, when dried herbs are used, combined in small muslin (cheesecloth) bags.

Calvados
An apple brandy made in the Normandy region, similar to Armagnac and Cognac.

Confit
Food that has been cooked in its own juices, to both flavour and preserve it. Sealed and stored in a cool place, confit can last for several months.

Crème fraîche
A thick and smooth sour cream. If you cannot find any in the shops, make your own by whisking 250 ml / 8 fl oz (1 cup) heavy (double) cream and 2 tablespoons buttermilk together in a bowl. Set the bowl in a larger bowl of hot water to bring the cream to room temperature, then remove, partially cover and let stand 8 to 24 hours, or until very thick. Stir well and refrigerate for up to 10 days.

Foie gras
The liver of a specially fattened goose or duck. It is a luxury item, considered by many to be a delicacy.

Grenadine
A dark red pomegranate-flavoured syrup used in drinks and desserts. Originally made from pomegranate fruits, grenadine is now more commonly made from other concentrated fruit juices.

Julienne
Method of food preparation in which food – usually vegetables – is cut into long thin strips.

Lardons
Small pieces of thick cut bacon, sold ready-chopped. If unavailable, a good substitute is thick rashers of bacon cut lengthways into strips and then into dice.

Marrons glacés
A French term meaning 'glazed chestnuts', these are chestnuts that have been soaked in a sugar syrup and flavoured with vanilla.

Nam pla (Thai fish sauce)
Nam pla is an essential ingredient in Vietnamese and Thai cooking, and is a salty fermented sauce made from small, whole fish. It can be used as a condiment, sauce and seasoning. It is available in supermarkets and specialist shops.

Pain d'épice
Translated as 'spice bread', pain d'épice can be described as a more savoury version of traditional gingerbread. In addition to ginger, it often includes some of the following flavours: cardamom, cloves, nutmeg and rum. See page 132 for the recipe.

Parfait
More usually used to describe a frozen French dessert, parfait can also refer to a meat, seafood or vegetable dish similar to pâté.

Pastis
A clear aniseed-flavoured liqueur and aperitif, similar to ouzo, with a high alcohol content. It is usually diluted with water before drinking, which turns it whitish and cloudy.

Pâté
French for 'pie', pâté refers to well-seasoned minced (ground) meat preparations that can be smooth or coarsely textured, and served hot or cold. Traditionally, 'pâté' refers to a dish that has been removed from the cooking dish, or terrine, before serving while 'terrine' refers to a dish served still in the mould; however the two terms now have become interchangeable.

Pig's caul
The thin, fatty membrane of the pig's stomach used to wrap and contain pâtés and terrines. To prevent the caul from tearing, you may need to soak the membrane in warm salted water before using.

Piment d'Espelette
The red pods of these peppers, grown in the Basque region in France, are threaded on cords and hung out to dry in the sun. They are then ground into powder or made into pastes. If unavailable, substitute hot paprika or New Mexico red chilli (chile) powder.

Pomelo
Native to Southeast Asia, this large citrus fruit varies between clear pale yellow to pink and red in colour and tastes like a sweet, mild grapefruit. An alternative to the pomelo is the pink grapefruit.

Praline paste
A baking item found in speciality baking shops. Made from almond or hazelnut butter and sugar, this thick paste is similar to peanut butter in texture.

Quatre épices
A finely ground 'four spice' mixture often including white pepper, nutmeg, ginger, cinnamon or cloves.

Quinoa (pronounced, keen-wah)
A small round grain native to the Andean region of Central America. When cooked, it has a light, fluffy texture and a delicate nutty flavour. Quinoa is rich in protein and is an alternative to rice and couscous.

Rilletes
Meat that has been slowly cooked in fat, shredded, then mixed with enough of the cooking fat to form a paste. After cooking it is packed into a terrine or ramekin and topped with a thin layer of fat. Rillettes will keep for several weeks in the refrigerator provided the fat seal is not broken.

Savory
A herb closely related to rosemary and thyme. There are two types – summer and winter. Both types have a strong flavour, similar to a cross between thyme and mint.

Sterilizing preserving jars
To sterilize your preserving jars before use, wash them well in warm soapy water. Rinse thoroughly and place in an oven for half an hour at 130°C / 250°F / Gas Mark ¼ to dry completely.

Sweetbreads
The thymus gland of veal, young beef, lamb and pork. Sweetbreads are available in specialist meat markets. Before being cooked, they should be soaked in several changes of water and the outer membrane removed.

Terrine
An earthenware cooking dish with vertical sides and a tightly fitting lid. By extension, the term also refers to food cooked in a terrine – traditionally a rich dish made from layered meat. Contemporary recipes now include a much wider variety of ingredients such as fish, cheese, vegetables and desserts.

Note

Unless otherwise stated, milk is assumed to be full fat.

Unless otherwise stated, eggs and individual vegetables and fruits are assumed to be medium.

Cooking times are for guidance only, as individual ovens vary. If using a fan oven, follow the manufacturer's instructions concerning oven temperatures.

Some recipes include raw or very lightly cooked eggs, foie gras or unpasteurized cheese. These should be avoided particularly by the elderly, infants, pregnant women, convalescents and anyone with an impaired immune system.

Both metric and imperial measures are used in this book. Follow one set of measurements throughout, not a mixture, as they are not interchangeable.

All spoon measurements are level.
1 teaspoon = 5 ml; 1 tablespoon = 15 ml.

Unless otherwise stated, all recipes are suitable for a standard 25 x 10 cm rectangular terrine.

Australian standard tablespoons are 20 ml, so Australian readers are advised to use 3 teaspoons in place of 1 tablespoon when measuring small quantities of flour, cornflour, etc.

Bon appétit!

Phaidon Press Limited
Regent's Wharf
All Saints Street
London N1 9PA

Phaidon Press Inc.
180 Varick Street
New York, NY 10014

www.phaidon.com

First published in English 2008
Reprinted 2011, 2013
©2008 Phaidon Press Limited

First published in French as
Vous prendrez bien un peu d'terrine?
by Marabout in 2005

ISBN 978 0 7148 4848 8

Translated from the French
by Mary Consonni

Photographs by Charlotte Lascève
Illustrations by Sonya Dyakova
Designed by Sonya Dyakova
with Susanne Olsson
Printed in China